MY DREAM

Memoirs of a one-of-a-kind disciple

George E. Vandeman

Pacific Press Publishing Association
Boise, Idaho
Oshawa, Ontario, Canada

Edited by Kenneth R. Wade
Designed by Tim Larson
Cover portrait by Ilyong Cha
Typeset in 12.5/14.5 Bookman

Library of Congress Cataloging-in-Publication
Data

Vandeman, George E.
　　My dream : memoirs of a one-of-a-kind
disciple / George E. Vandeman.
　　　　p.　cm.
　　ISBN 0-8163-1305-9
　　1. Vandeman, George E. 2. Seventh-day
Adventists—United States—Clergy—Biogra-
phy. 3. Evangelists—United States—Biogra-
phy. 4. "It is written" (Television program)
I. Title.
BX6193.V359A3　1995
286.7'092—dc20
[B]　　　　　　　　　　　　　　95-38961
　　　　　　　　　　　　　　　　CIP

96 97 98 99 • 5 4 3 2

Dedication

I lovingly dedicate
My Dream
to my precious wife, Nellie,
who helped to make it all possible.

Contents

Foreword

by Dennis O'Flaherty

If you had asked me, five years ago, if I thought it likely that I would someday be writing a foreword to the memoirs of one of our century's great evangelists, let alone be proud to call such a man my friend, I would have had to smile. Though I had been a churchgoing Christian since I was a boy, I had spent most of my adult life in the academic world and writing for the entertainment industry. To me, the activities of evangelists were something remote and slightly mystifying. As an academic, my specialty had been Russian political history, and the "believers" in my daily readings were grimly dedicated revolutionaries, almost all of them proud atheists and materialists. Moreover, the last decade of my university life was spent at Oxford, in an atmosphere where undue enthusiasm of any kind—let alone religious enthusiasm—was regarded with an arched eyebrow and a patronizing smile.

After I made my move from the academic world to the entertainment industry, the aims and activities of evangelists remained somewhere at the far horizon of my attention. It wasn't that people in the "biz" are nearly as irreligious and immoral as the sensationalist media paint them, but rather that—as in any part of American big-business culture—when people are busy from dawn to dusk chasing the "almighty dollar," they tend to forget that the use of the word *almighty* in this context is supposed to be a joke.

It was by a seeming coincidence (in which I can now sense the hand of Providence) that a friendship with one of Hollywood's most venerable screenwriters brought me to the doorstep of the Adventist Media Center, where the president, Glenn Aufderhar, was looking for someone to help realize a long-standing plan to make an animated version of Arthur Maxwell's *Bible Story*. I had spent years writing scripts for kids' cartoons and had often been frustrated by the impossibility of getting any kind of serious content into them; here was a project and a man—for I warmed to Glenn at once—that I could really enjoy working with! At last, the activities of evangelists had come into clear view for me, as close up as friendship can bring them; for Glenn and his warm and thoughtful wife, Barbara, shared the Bible and their time with us until my wife,

Mel, and I were finally baptized into the fellowship of the Camarillo, California, Seventh-day Adventist Church. But perhaps I'm skipping just a bit too far ahead, as this only happened after I had met and become friends with George Vandeman—in Moscow!

For me, this was a truly providential happening. For two decades, I had dreamed of going back to Moscow, where I had spent one of my happiest years as a researcher at the university. As life developed, there seemed no reasonable excuse for such a long and expensive trip, yet here, suddenly, was Glenn Aufderhar asking if I could consider putting my Russian background at the church's service by going to Moscow! The occasion was Mark Finley's great Moscow crusade, and the *It Is Written* team needed someone from home who could speak enough Russian to act as a sort of all-purpose assistant.

One thing led to another, and I found myself back amongst my Russian friends, this time in an incredibly exciting context for someone who had been close to both the Jewish and the Christian "undergrounds" in the old days. For now, instead of the cloak-and-dagger atmosphere that used to surround worship in Russia, you had an openness and excitement that were reminiscent of the early Christian spirit described in Acts. Not only that, I found myself with a group of people whose spiritual profile with the Russian people was amazingly high, thanks in large part—as you might have guessed—to the activities of one George Vandeman. I'm sure Mark

Finley—whose crusade was enormously successful on its own merits—won't mind my saying that
people were repeatedly asking for "*Gospodin
Vandeman*," whose face and voice had become
indelibly identified with the *It Is Written* experience for them over the years.

It was a deeply exciting moment when George
finally appeared in Moscow's Olympic Sports
Stadium to pass on the torch of *It Is Written* leadership to Mark and a great moment for me, personally, when I was finally able to meet George.
I can remember the moment well: the crusade
workers were billeted at a serviceable, but far-
from-deluxe, hotel on the outskirts of the city,
and the hard-nosed staff there were more accustomed to dealing with Mafiosi from the
Caucasus than with a bunch of American evangelists. Generally, their manner with people who
couldn't speak Russian (not to mention those
who could) made the traditional U.S. "get outa
here, kid; ya bother me!" seem like the height of
civilized good manners. Yet here was one of the
Baikal's "iron maidens" trying to explain herself
with the greatest gentleness to a silver-haired
gent who clearly didn't understand a word.

The silver-haired gent (guess who?) turned to
me and asked in that famous voice: "Do you think
you could help us?" I'm convinced that George
could get the statues in the local park to climb
off their pedestals and pitch in if he asked them
to, and *I* certainly wasn't going to say No—so
this began an acquaintance that ripened into
friendship and has continued to be intertwined

with our own Adventist experience, since we're lucky enough to have George and Nellie, as well as their daughter, Connie, as fellow members of the Camarillo Church.

As time has passed and I have learned more about *It Is Written*, I have come to appreciate George's work even more, observing his achievements from the viewpoint of someone who earns his daily bread working for the media and sharing the media's restless drive to find out just what it takes to unlock the sympathies of the vast and always mysterious viewing audience. The answer, when you watch George and listen to him, is simple: *genuineness*. In a world where everything is artifice, George's transparent goodness and sincerity shine like a beacon, and nothing could be more important when you're bringing people a message as important as the one George has been spreading for all these years.

I was interested to read a study that was prepared for the Media Center board a few years back by the Magid Company, a tough-minded group of showbiz analysts, in which they analyzed the strengths and weaknesses of *It Is Written* from a media point of view. To spare you a lot of learned verbiage, it all boiled down to one thing: "George Vandeman is a tremendous communicator." What makes a great "communicator"? A smooth voice? Good lighting? Lots of publicity? A legion of dime-a-dozen "communicator wannabes" have all that but don't have the quality of *heart* that is George's. This couldn't be said better than it was recently by Dr. Benjamin Carson in his book *Think Big*, published by Zondervan publishers:

> Another outstanding individual who has impressed me because of his closeness to God is George Vandeman. For more than forty years, George has preached on radio and TV on a program called *It Is Written*. His broadcast is seen not only everywhere in this country, but throughout Europe, and was beamed at the Eastern Bloc nations long before *glasnost*. He is now being heard in China.
>
> Yet, with all his accomplishments—and they are many—he is still a humble man. Because George knows where his ability comes from, he does everything quietly and without fanfare. He is softspoken, practical, nonjudgmental, and one of the nicest guys I have ever met.

All I can say to that is "Hear! Hear!" Now read on and enjoy meeting George for yourselves.

Introduction

by Connie Vandeman Jeffery

One Sunday afternoon in January 1995, our family gathered at Mom and Dad's Camarillo home to celebrate my brother George's birthday. Because of our extended family, we get together on nearly a monthly basis for various holidays and birthdays. After a lovely dinner and gift opening, I mentioned to Dad an idea I had discussed with Dennis O'Flaherty. Dennis had thought that now would be an excellent time for my father to write his memoirs, and I agreed wholeheartedly. The entire family seized on the idea with enthusiasm, and as Dad quietly thought about it after dinner, you could almost see the sparkle in his eyes grow brighter by the minute.

My brother George and I had been concerned about Dad's health following his "retirement" from *It Is Written*. Although he continues to travel for the program and to have occasional speaking engagements, it is becoming increasingly evident that he is indeed approaching his eightieth year and must slow down. This idea of writing his story, his memoirs, somehow gave him a renewed sense of purpose, a raison d'être. Mother was just as enthusiastic about the project. She had been wanting him to write something like this for years, but somehow there had never been time. Now, he has time, and his mind and memory are as sharp as they have ever been.

It has been such a pleasure to watch him go through the process of writing and rewriting and remembering the remarkable events of the past fifty-seven years of his ministry and seventy-nine years of his life. Mother has provided invaluable help to him in recalling dates and important events and in gathering the priceless photos in this book. I have tried to keep reminding Dad that this is *his* story—his dream. Being the man he is, it is sometimes difficult for him to elaborate on the truly great moments, the pride of his accomplishments, and the fulfillment of his dreams. He is, at the very core, a deeply humble man who gives every bit of credit to his Lord and Saviour, Jesus Christ.

As his daughter, perhaps I can say a few things about him that he cannot say himself. I have always been so very proud of him as a father. My childhood friends used to ask me if Dad was the same man at home as he was on television. The answer was always Yes! The same softspoken, self-deprecating, strong, but gentle man they saw on *It Is Written* was the man I called Dad. He didn't have a public and a private persona. We could always count on him to be the same, a constant in an ever-changing world.

I'll never forget the one and only spanking he gave me. I was about seven years old and had done something particularly naughty. He felt some punishment was in order, but he could hardly bring himself to ever-so-gently spank, or rather pat, my backside as tears rolled down his cheeks. "This hurts me more than it hurts you," he said over and over again. That was certainly a true statement, since I don't recall the "spanking" hurting me at all! I only felt sorry that it seemed to hurt him so much. So, of course, the punishment worked.

My father was, is, and always will be the most deeply spiritual person I have ever known. He is a man who has always firmly believed in the power of prayer. I can't begin to count the times I have walked into his study early in the morning to find him on his knees, his head resting in his hands. When I was very young, I would sometimes just watch him as the minutes ticked by and wonder what in the world he could be talking to God about all that time. I used to go over and poke him occasionally to see if he had fallen asleep on his knees. He would patiently look up and tell me that he was almost finished. And after his private devotions, we would have morning worship as a family. I won't forget how he has always talked to God as a friend.

Although Dad makes no claims to be an expert on marriage and the family, his fifty-seven-year marriage stands as a testament to that sacred institution. And what an extraordinary and loving union it has been! Over the years, in this chaotic and uncertain world, the two focal points around which my parents have centered their lives have been their undying faith in their Lord and their unconditional love for each other. What an inspiration and example they have been for all of us.

There have been many ups and downs, many joys and many sorrows in Dad's life. The joy has outweighed the sorrow by a long shot. Through it all, his dream has remained intact and grown stronger with each passing year. By God's grace, he has served Him for nearly eighty years and helped to carry His message all over this planet. And by God's grace he will continue to proclaim His message and be a living, inspiring example for many years to come. It is up to you and me to carry on his *dream.*

One

It Happened in Moscow

I was seated in Moscow in the usual bleak office surroundings of a giant pre-glasnost television complex—no frills—gray decor—a frowning picture of Lenin on the back wall. Through the window, I could see the famed Ostankino Tower—the world's second-highest free-standing television tower—rising into the sky.

The surroundings did little to boost my courage, but with visit after visit in that pre-Gorbachev and Yeltsin era, I was getting used to the austerity.

It was an awesome moment in my life. The gentleman across the table was the general manager of Soviet national television. He looked me squarely in the eye and said decisively, "*I am asking you to be the moral voice for my country.*"

The moral voice for 350 million people! Was that what God had in mind? I am only human; I have my share of misgivings and recognize my limitations. Yet was I not taught, "God's ideal for His children is higher than the highest human thought can reach" (*The Desire of Ages*, 311)?

Television!—our last-day miracle of communication. An overwhelming avenue of persuasion. And was I not called to preach the gospel to *every* nation, kindred, tongue and people? (see Revelation 14:6.)

Well, maybe this is what God had in mind when He shaped the circumstances to place me, at birth, where radio and television in the Adventist Church would be nurtured.

The announcement was simple enough. The "blessed event" notice read,

> Nina Royce Vandeman gave birth to George Edward at 9:00 a.m. on October 21, 1916, and presented this son to his father, Herbert A. Vandeman.

Could it be providence that Nina Vandeman, my mother, with Herbert, my father, were co-workers with H. M. S. Richards, the patriarch of radio broadcasting, who profoundly influenced a generation in the church?

The scene was Pueblo, Colorado, my birthplace. Conference officials placed these two young workers together. Dad was older in years but younger in the faith. Harold Richards was younger in years but older in the message—

which proved to be a very wise arrangement. The two became pioneers in radio broadcasting at just the right moment in Adventist history.

I have always considered it an honor to have been bounced on Harold Richard's knee—a practice that he and I reminisced about occasionally even up to the time of his ninetieth birthday.

Harold Richards, of course, became the unquestioned champion of radio programming. Dad took a lesser role, but one that was very meaningful to me.

When I was still small, he took me aside and taught me to build a simple crystal radio set. It consisted of a tiny crystal, "cat's whiskers" (a small wire to scan the crystal), and a pair of crude earphones. It worked! That day, I heard the President of the United States, Calvin Coolidge, give one of his early radio addresses. And I was impressed.

Add to this the advantage of having a father "obsessed" with the urge to develop radio broadcasting in the Adventist Church. It was no accident. He traveled from the east to Emmanuel Missionary College in southern Michigan, where a young visionary by the name of John Fetzer persuaded the administration of the college to invest in a radio station to air a series of programs each week on a fifty-thousand-watt transmitter—fifty thousand watts! Yes, but remember that this was long before the government controlled radio wave power. For some time, that station controlled the airwaves in that part of Michigan and northern Indiana.

However, John Fetzer soon wearied of organizational constraints and committee control and left Emmanuel Missionary College to start a station in Kalimazoo, Michigan, just fifty miles north of the college. John Fetzer's radio exploits soon developed into dominant television coverage, with expansion into other interests, not the least of which was ownership of the Detroit Tigers baseball team.

John never quite lost his early convictions. He asked for H. M. S. Richards to conduct his mother's funeral some years ago. I suppose eternity will have to settle the quandary of his own convictions.

Eventually, Allentown, Pennsylvania, became Dad's fertile radio seed-sowing ground. There he discovered a homespun technical genius by the name of Heinbach who built a radio station in his own house on Tilghman Street. His living room served as a studio. The third floor, or rather enlarged attic, contained his controls. Often I accompanied Dad to hear those first radio sermons. Heinbach would confide in my father with a wry smile, "Vandeman, when the preachers in my living room don't interest me, I turn them off and give the audience some nice music. But I've never cut you off once."

Well, from that crude beginning, that station, WCBA, grew into splendidly equipped studios in the heart of the city. I also remember the first owner of this new station, Bryan Musselman. He was a Mennonite minister. Not the kind of Mennonite who drove buggies, but rather, modern automobiles. And one who wore ties instead of buttonless shirts. He was always friendly and helpful to my dad, till at last Father's radio venture, which covered several years, moved quietly and silently into history.

And all the while, this teenager listened!

The loss of my dad was a very sad occasion. I was aware, of course, that having his personal presence with me could not continue indefinitely. But, nevertheless, I shall always cherish the things he did that helped me to accomplish my dreams of service.

I visited him frequently while he was in the hospital, and he and I warmly appreciated those times together. So much we could not say in words was nevertheless understood between us. How I have wished again and again that he could have rejoiced at the fruit of his prayers and the counsel he gave me. Eternity will handle that matter, I am sure. But let me tell you how thankful I am that he did live to know the following details. And maybe in the telling you can grasp a little of the story in the rest of the book.

He knew of my first year at Emmanuel Missionary College. I was yet unmarried and restless to be on with preaching. During that year, I contracted, for the sum of $15.00, a weekly radio broadcast in nearby Elkhart, Indiana.

He knew of my graduation. After I had been away from school for two years, conducting evangelistic meetings, older and wiser leaders saw that if I did not receive thorough training, my ministry would be severely limited. My wife,

Nellie, will never forget the straight, authoritative finger of the wife of the Michigan Conference president, Carlyle B. Haynes. "Young lady," she admonished, "you get that young man back to school. He has a great future, but he must finish his education." So back to school we went.

For the next two years, I managed to do some pastoral evangelistic work along with my class work. After I graduated, the president of the college called me to teach. I was assigned to teach evangelism, speech, and a few other subjects and built the first radio and recording studio for the institution.

Dad knew about my call from the classroom to the General Conference Ministerial Association in Washington, D.C. At thirty-three, I was the youngest worker called to that august building. I felt somewhat uncomfortable working with these "graybeards," as I at first humorously thought of them. But they were very kind and somewhat proud of their "youngster." They evidently believed in me and immediately assigned me to the interesting task of visiting all of our colleges to encourage the vision of ministerial students.

He knew about the brethren sending me on my first overseas assignment to India. When I learned that the cost of a ticket to and from India was no different from one around the world, which do you suppose I chose? Yes, you guessed it—around the world! That's how I first visited Palestine. I arrived there in the midst of a bitter and protracted war and climbed over the barbed-wire fence from one side to the other just outside of old Jerusalem. This was at the time when Israel was first declared a state. Later in this book you will learn the fascinating details that led to my sitting with the VIPs in the Jerusalem Convention Hall, with earphones bringing me an excellent English translation of this historic event.

Yes, he knew and was gratified for all this and more before we laid him to rest from his labors.

Two

On a
Friday Night

I t was on a Friday night that I shook my fist at God. Five minutes before it happened, you might have written me down as a decent, respectable, promising young man with drive and dedication and—well, going somewhere. But inside I was riot and revolt and rebellion and civil war and guilt—all rolled into a bored, frustrated kid, generation gap and all.

My father was a minister. He understood people. He helped people. He won people. And I watched and listened and was deeply impressed. I learned even before my teens that sermons do not come from mental discipline, wide reading, and scholastic achievement alone—however essential these may be—but from life.

There wasn't a trace of phoniness in my father or in my family or in my home church, as far as

I can remember. That was one problem I did not have. Rather than being turned away from religion by people who didn't live it, I was constantly being drawn back to it by the compelling demonstration of God's power to change lives—drawn back, I say, while I was trying to escape.

You see, I had this hang-up about freedom. If you think youth rebelliousness originated in the sixties, you're mistaken. Just like kids today, I didn't want to be restricted. I didn't want to be fenced in. I didn't want to be inhibited. I wanted to make up my own rules. As a minister's son, I was being watched. And I didn't want to be watched.

But it was more than that. Early in my teens, gnawing away at my restless mind, came the first faint suggestion that God might someday call me into the ministry. I confess that the idea surprised me. And it was even more of a surprise to those who knew me.

These were convictions I was determined to stifle. However appealing my home background and however insistent the call of God to my young heart, I determined to silence the inner voice and discover life for myself. I would safeguard my future security by preparing to be a civil engineer. I'm not sure whether I really wanted to be a civil engineer or whether I just didn't want to be a minister. I knew, of course, that if God wants a man to go to Nineveh—wherever that Nineveh may be—no other place will do. And besides, I had a lurking suspicion that the thing I was fighting was the thing I really wanted. I was all mixed up and unwilling to admit it to anyone, much less to myself.

I tremble to think of what I so narrowly escaped. No, there were no brushes with the law. There was nothing in my conduct revolting to society or even embarrassing to my family. No scandals to live down.

It seems to me that conversion is easier for a man whose sins are etched in deep scarlet. Such a man, unless he has completely silenced the voice of God to his heart, knows where he stands. He knows he needs God. I didn't.

I was gripped by something worse than scarlet sin. Mine were *respectable sins.* I was lost in the church. And don't let anybody tell you it can't happen. Because it can. Please believe me. It is altogether possible to accept a theory, to be satisfied with a form of religion, and yet to be lost— lost in the church!

Oh, I would go to church and hear a sermon, and I would be concerned. I would read the newspaper and see events following Bible prediction like a blueprint, and I would be troubled. But when I tackled my own natural weaknesses— and sometimes I did want to tackle them—I was completely helpless.

I think that was the real problem. Religion, at least my experience with it, seemed to be very weak on the *how.* And of what use is a religion that doesn't work—that does not satisfy?

I became so weary of boredom and defeat that I tried to run away from conscience. But, thank God, conscience—unless you kill it—will never let you go!

Finally, I could stand it no longer. It was a Friday evening, and I was seated in a meeting where my father was speaking. There he stood—my ideal of a minister, my ideal of a man.

He was speaking to the entire congregation, not to me in particular. But every word he said cut like a knife. I got up and walked out of the meeting and moved restlessly into the shadows. I shall never forget those moments. In that still summer evening, looking up past the trees into God's own sky, I actually shook my fist at the heavens and said, "Holy Spirit, leave me! And don't ever come back!"

Thank God, that prayer was never answered! But breathing those words, the shock of having said them, did something to me. At least the words were prayer, though bitter in their defiance.

This was the climax to a long series of events in which the tempter had been overstepping himself. And now, by my own defiant words, I was thoroughly shocked. For the first time, I saw the fine print on the devil's contract. And I decided to break it.

Little did I dream that I was standing on the threshold of a transforming experience that would dwarf all my former visions of personal happiness and satisfaction. I was to learn a secret that would forever change my own restless soul.

And that is what I want to share with you in these pages. Not just my own story. Rather, growing out of it, building upon its discoveries, focusing from many angles, I want to introduce to you Jesus, my Lord and Saviour. I want to talk with you about some of the questions that so perplexed and confused and haunted me. I want to do this because I know that the questions that tapped so insistently at my mind must have tapped at your mind too. For really, we are all alike. The problems don't change with generations—only the scene, only the vocabulary.

Now, back to my story. After that confrontation under the stars, I set out at once to reconstruct my life, to set my house in order, to realign my thinking and my goals. I knew what was right. *Information* was not enough. I needed *demonstration*—in my own life. But for many months, the secret I was seeking seemed to evade me.

What troubled me was that no matter how vigorously I tried to make a change, I repeatedly failed. Yet when I asked older Christians how to rechannel my life, how to break the power of wrong habit—and I must have asked the wrong ones—their counsel was usually just this: "Try harder."

Listen. If friends or counselors tell you to try harder, tell them they are wrong! I know they may not call it *trying*. They may call it self-discipline. They may offer you some psychological formula, some new secret for tapping a power they say is within you. They may suggest some involvement in the problems of society. But it's the same old *trying*—trying to lift yourself by your own power. And it doesn't work!

You can try until you are weary. You can try

until you are worn-out. But still your weaknesses will mock you. Trying only focuses attention upon yourself. What you need is a power outside yourself. It is only the power of the living God that can change and transform.

The only way to get into the kingdom of God is to *be born* into it—by a miracle. It is just that simple. But I didn't understand.

And so, although it sounded a little too much like self-hypnosis, I whipped up my determination again, flexed my muscles, and made another try. But before long, my willpower relaxed, and I found myself right back where I had started. This meant discouragement. And if there was anything I didn't need, it was discouragement. Or did I? At least it jarred me into action.

Evidently something was wrong here. I dropped to my knees. I opened the Bible. For if this business of Christian living was genuine, there would have to be a more adequate demonstration of it in my life. Certainly there ought to be more to the gospel than another chance after every defeat.

Now came the surprise. As I opened the Scriptures, I found little emphasis on self-discipline. Instead, I found such words as these: "Can the Ethiopian change his skin, or the leopard his spots? then may ye also do good, that are accustomed to do evil" (Jeremiah 13:23).

And I found the words of Jesus: "Do men gather grapes of thorns, or figs of thistles? . . . Neither can a corrupt tree bring forth good fruit" (Matthew 7:16-18).

No wonder it could not be done by rigid mental effort! No wonder all my noble resolutions were about as strong as ropes of sand!

And then imagine how I felt as I discovered in Romans 7 a description of the very conflict I kept experiencing over and over like a broken record. I had only the familiar King James Version then, of course. But the translation by Dr. Phillips makes it so graphically clear:

> My own behaviour baffles me. For I find myself doing what I really loathe but not doing what I really want to do. . . . I often find that I have the will to do good, but not the power. That is, I don't accomplish the good I set out to do, and the evil I don't really want to do I find I am always doing. . . . I am in hearty agreement with God's Law so far as my inner self is concerned. But then I find another law in my bodily members, which is in continual conflict with the Law which my mind approves, and makes me a prisoner to the law of sin which is inherent in my mortal body. . . . It is an agonising situation, and who can set me free from the prison of this mortal body? I thank God there is a way out through Jesus Christ our Lord (Romans 7:15-25, Phillips, revised edition).

How could Paul have described my confusion more accurately? It was as if he had been looking over my shoulder!

But there was a way out! That brought courage. Evidently the difficulty was in my own sinful nature. I began to understand why it is that a person sins. I realized that this planet is in rebellion against a good and loving God and that a fallen, corrupt, degenerate nature has been passed on from generation to generation. Sin and disobedience and rebellion have so warped and undermined the perfect nature that God originally bestowed upon Adam and Eve that it is utterly impossible for anyone, in his or her own strength, to live for God.

No wonder I had made so little progress in solving my problems. How could it be otherwise, so long as my fundamental nature was unchanged? I had attempted to cover conflict and defeat with outward discipline. I had been content to keep my objectionable traits of character while I grasped frantically for grace and poise and personality to cover them up. But I was missing the real point.

How often I had seen it in others! For it is one thing for a hostess to keep sweet and charming at a social function when a guest soils her lovely gown—outwardly calm while she is burning inside. It is one thing for an employer to be courteous to a bungling worker, a blundering customer, when influence and reputation are at stake—though all the while hate burns in his heart. But it is quite another thing to have a power inside that will take away the hate and the burning.

I saw that patching up the outside could never

heal the inside. I could not cover defeat with culture or weakness with personality. I must have a power that could go deeper than that or forever live with a mocking heart.

But light began to dawn. Hope sprang up as I read such words as are found in 1 Thessalonians 5:24: "Faithful is he that calleth you, who also will do it." *He* promises to do it. But I had been trying to do it myself!

And 2 Peter 1:4 solved the problem: "Whereby are given unto us exceeding great and precious promises: that by these ye might be partakers of the divine nature."

I saw now why simply working at it had proved so disappointing. Evidently God had wanted to do something deep and fundamental within me, and I had not permitted it. It was a new nature that I needed.

A friend helped me one day with a very simple illustration. Let us suppose, he suggested, that a timber wolf should watch and admire the habits of a flock of peaceful sheep and decide that an animal ought to live that way. Suppose he attempts now to live just as a sheep lives. Wouldn't that wolf have a difficult time? Wouldn't he be likely to slip back into his old way of life? Grass might seem quite tasteless as he remembered feeding on some carcass.

But suppose that God, by a miracle known only to the Creator, should transplant into the wolf the nature of a sheep. Then would it be difficult to live like a sheep? Not at all!

Well, it helped me. The possibility described in

33

2 Corinthians 5:17 now made sense. How had I missed the very thing I needed? Listen: "If any man be in Christ, he is a new creature: old things are passed away; behold, all things are become new."

I stood in wonder before the utter simplicity of God's plan. How could it have been so difficult to grasp? Did it need to be? Would a God so anxious to save us reveal the way in words we could not understand? Surely not.

Unfortunately, the language of religion, with its familiar vocabulary, like the repetitious chiming of a bell, sometimes just doesn't register. We hear the words so often that we scarcely hear them at all. How many times my father had tried to tell me the secret! But I never got the message.

It was amazing how all the Scripture statements on this subject now seemed to fall into place, as in an almost-completed puzzle. The incident related in John 3 now became more vital to me than I had ever dreamed possible. You remember that Nicodemus—a man thoroughly respected, highly trained, possessed of a dignity and culture rarely seen in those times—came to Jesus by night. And there under a Judean sky, the Saviour of humanity kindly but forcefully probed to the heart of his problem as He said, "Except a man be born again, he cannot see the kingdom of God."

Strong words, these. And Nicodemus did not understand. He questioned the possibility of rebirth. But Jesus pressed His point home again:

"Except a man be born of water and of the Spirit, he cannot enter into the kingdom of God."

My wonder deepened at those words of Jesus. Evidently such a transformation is possible. But how could it be brought about? God led me to an answer—one that had been there all the time: "Which were born, not of blood, nor of the will of the flesh, nor of the will of man, but of God" (John 1:13).

The new birth was not something that could come about through the will of man. No wonder I had failed! No wonder willpower wasn't enough!

True, I had changed direction. I had decided to break my contract with rebellion. I had faced the unpleasant task of confession. I had felt the remorse that Peter must have felt when he denied his Lord. I had come to the place where I could say, "I am sorry. No one else is responsible. I am to blame. God help me!"

All this was opening the floodgates for the change I needed—the new birth. But nothing I did could bring it about.

Unquestionably, I needed a miracle. And did I—George Vandeman, master of my own future, I thought—did I have to submit to a miracle? Evidently. For the person who is attempting to remake himself without God is attempting an impossibility. He is attempting something that requires creative power. And no one but God is equipped for that.

The Christian life is not simply a modification or an improvement or a repairing of the old. Rather, it is a transformation of a person's nature. It is an act of creation—making a new person.

Since the day I discovered that secret, my deepest satisfaction has been to see the new light in the eyes of men and women as that priceless truth dawns.

It all came about so effortlessly. And I had tried so hard!

Listen: "No one sees the hand that lifts the burden, or beholds the light descend from the courts above. The blessing comes when by faith the soul *surrenders* itself to God. *Then* that power which no human eye can see creates a new being in the image of God" (*The Desire of Ages*, 173, emphasis supplied).

No one sees the hand. But the miracle is there!

Tongue cannot tell it. Pen cannot write it—the peace this transaction brings to the human breast. This is the transforming secret that was to dwarf every youthful dream into insignificance. I learned it the hard way. But I learned it never to forget.

Let me take you back to that night when I stood in the shadows, looking up at the stars. Had I been examined that night on the theory of truth, I would have passed with flying colors. In fact, if my father had been called away by some emergency, I think I could have preached his sermon with clarity. But it was not theory I needed—or clarity. It was life!

I knew then and there that if ever these lips or this pen were commissioned to share truth with others, power must attend the sharing, or it would accomplish nothing. I knew even that night the terrible responsibility of the ministry. For no man or woman is ever the same after they have confronted the claims of Christ.

I knew then, as I know much better now, that it is possible for people with eternal destinies at stake to accept a theory of truth and yet lose out. For without the transforming process that comes alone through divine power, the original tendencies to sin are left in the heart in all their strength, there to forge new chains and impose a slavery that the power of men or women can never break.

I had so narrowly escaped such a slavery that I determined no one within the hearing of my voice would ever step back into life unaware of its danger. God help the one who rests passively and unafraid under the shadow of a superficial profession, an outward cloak of religion! They are the people I sincerely pray my ministry has helped.

I realize now that the struggle of that night under the stars was in reality the beginning of my ministry—and the reason for it. God knew that the real desire of that lonely, restless heart was just the opposite of the words that escaped those lips. The desperate cry of the soul—that His Spirit might *never* leave—is the prayer He heard that night. And forever I thank God!

Three

I Learned
the Hard Way

"Was God Ever a Teenager?"
"How to Burn Your Candle"
"Untying the Knot"
"Happiness Wall to Wall"
"When Wounds Won't Heal"

All of these programs and a half dozen more were presented through the years on *It Is Written*, on the subject of home and marriage. As you can imagine, our programs on these topics brought an unusually good response. Although most people know that my staff and I must conduct extensive research before speaking on these practical matters, many viewers would certainly conclude that I was an expert in this important field of the home and family.

But the truth is, I have had to learn many vital lessons the hard way. For instance, I've often been keenly aware of my failing to give my own precious children the *quality time* they so much needed during their growing-up years. In the early days of the Bill Gothard seminars, Nellie and I attended a session. One of the lectures described fathers who put their work ahead of their families. The speaker even said that if any present were guilty of this, they should ask their children to forgive them. That lecture really hit home.

Later, when I spoke to my son George, the eldest, about my deepest heartfelt regrets, he said, "It's true, Dad, that we would like to have been with you more during our early years. But don't be too hard on yourself. If it hadn't been for your work, we would never have been able to travel as we did all over the country, to live in England for two years, or to meet our relatives in Norway."

I believe that my dear wife, Nellie, deserves most of the credit for George feeling this way. She was always there for the children. She stayed close to them when I felt I could not do so as much as I wanted.

Nellie was athletically inclined—a seasoned basketball player in her high-school years—which made it easier for her to identify with the boys. And boys were all we had in the early years. Her upbeat Norwegian vigor and humor helped tremendously. We all love her dearly for it.

Her mother, Grandma Johnson, helped too.

I remember when the boys and Grandma, Nellie, and I were driving across the high Sierras en route to the West Coast. It was then that Grandma lamented in her broken English, "The *attitude* gets me up here." We all had a good laugh as we explained to her the difference between *attitude* and *altitude*. The family really never let her live that one down. She chuckled every time she heard it. I even mentioned the incident at her funeral.

On another occasion, while traveling together as a family with Grandma, Nellie and I found ourselves in a disagreement. Evidently I was in the wrong and was reticent to admit it. Grandma, struggling for words, admonished, "You do better, won't you, Yorge?" Everyone in the car roared in laughter—at her uniquely kind concern. That broke the tension. And of course I learned a valuable lesson about not taking myself so seriously. I learned that laughing at ourselves would do us all a lot of good. Honesty brings its own healing—healing that can level the playing ground for all of us.

Let me back up a little and tell you about how it all got started. I have already told you how Nellie's mother added to the joy of our home. After all, Nellie was a Johnson from Beloit, Wisconsin, where there were 187 Johnsons listed in the phone book—that was the substantial Norwegian family tree from which my Nellie came. And I have always been proud of that heritage.

And now I want Nellie to tell you in her own words some deeply significant things that happened to her and that led to our meeting at Emmanuel Missionary College in the summer of 1937.

Thank you, George. Since George has been talking about my mother, I would like to tell you some things about her. My mother became an Adventist when I was about nine years old. She attended a tent meeting in Beloit, Wisconsin, and was baptized into the church. My father did not join the church, but neither did he oppose it. A number of Norwegian friends joined with her. Four of the younger children—I am the fourth of seven children—began going to Sabbath School and church with Mother, and we occasionally went to the Wisconsin camp meeting. I was baptized at the camp meeting in Portage, Wisconsin, when I was twelve years of age. During my high-school years, I drifted away from the church. After graduating in 1935, I was able to get a very good job in the office of one of the large manufacturing firms in town. Even though I had a very happy and eventful life, there was something that I was missing. In fact, at that time I was beginning to lose interest in the things of the world.

Then in the spring of 1937, on Easter Sunday, I was in an accident, a head-on collision that could have taken my life. This caused me to think very seriously about my future. Strong convictions came to me that I must make a change. So in June of that year I felt compelled to go to camp meeting. I asked the pastor of the church if I could ride with him to the campground. I just couldn't get enough of the meetings— I went to every one of them. The Sabbath-morning sermon touched my heart, and when a call was made, I went forward with tears in my eyes. One of the pastors came to my side, and after lunch he took me to the Emmanuel Missionary College (EMC) recruiting tent. He introduced me to Dr. Harold McCumber, who taught history at the college. We had a long visit. He was determined that I must get to EMC that fall and that he would do everything he could to help me get there. So he came to Beloit and visited with my mother and father. They agreed that I should go to EMC, and they would have liked to help. But I knew that I would have to work my own way.

Dr. McCumber soon informed me that he had arranged for part-time work for me in the College Wood Products office, but I would have to come by August 1. Of course, I was delighted. So within two weeks I quit my job with only $100 saved, packed my suitcase, and made my way to EMC.

It was like a dream fulfilled to realize I was there at Emmanuel Missionary

College. I could hardly believe it. Little did I realize what this school year held in store for me. Both George and I have always felt that aside from the leading of the Lord, Dr. McCumber gets the credit for bringing us together. How grateful we are to him.

Thanks, Nellie. The school year of 1937-38 was a busy one. In addition to my college studies, with the encouragement of the Religion Department, I began a fifteen-minute weekly radio program in nearby Elkhart, Indiana. I was also conducting Sunday-night evangelistic meetings there in a rented hall. I happened to meet Nellie in the college store later that year. I immediately noticed she was friendly and outgoing, so I invited her to assist in these Sunday-night meetings.

She came, and the next day I asked her how she liked it. "Wonderful," she said. "I enjoyed every minute of it." I am sure that I failed to hide my admiration of her as I told her that I wanted her to be a *permanent* member of the team. So she joined the other students who helped in the Sabbath and Sunday-night meetings. That was the beginning of a growing attraction for each other. And as the school year was drawing to a close, I confided in her my loving intention to deepen that relationship.

Fortunately, Nellie and a friend were assigned to the Elkhart area to canvass (work as colporteurs) for the summer months. This made it possible for her to attend and help at all of the meetings. Nellie lived with a lovely couple who seemed to take great pleasure in our budding courtship.

Nellie was anxious for me to meet her parents, so with some trepidation I visited her family and found them gracious and happy for the prospective union. I then took Nellie to the Michigan camp meeting to meet my parents. They were extremely pleased. My mother even said, "Now I don't have to worry about George anymore." We were both nearly twenty-two years of age at the time.

Back in Elkhart, one evening when no meeting was scheduled, I dropped by the house where Nellie was staying to have my sermon outline typed. I found her ironing downstairs in the basement. There in the stark surroundings of a typical Midwestern basement, I smiled and said, "Nellie, aren't we taking something for granted?"

"What do you mean?" was the cautious response.

"Marriage, sweetheart, that's what I mean." Now you would understand that I may have kissed her before. But you can be very sure I did then. But the wedding, when and how should it be planned? You see, the conference officials had asked if I would be willing to stay out of school for a year or two to follow up the many interests that had developed. Nellie was a bit hesitant, but we decided that the only wise course was to proceed with our wedding. And that sacred event took place on October 2, 1938, in the South Bend, Indiana, Church. My father officiated. You can see a photograph of that most important occasion in our lives on the first page of the picture section of this book.

Nellie and I became happy parents on January 16, 1940, when God gave us George, our first son. He was born in Muncie, Indiana, while Nellie and I were holding a series of tent meetings. Nellie and I and our two lady Bible workers were living in small tents behind the big one. One day a violent storm played havoc with that three-poled tent structure and it started to come down. Now picture, if you can, George, his two lady Bible workers, and his *pregnant* wife scurrying madly about, attempting to save the huge tent. We failed, of course. Down it came over the piano, platform, and audience seating.

Fortunately, kind neighbors and helpful church members rose to the occasion and managed to repair the canvas. If I remember correctly, we lost only two night meetings of the series. *But we gained a fine son, George*—probably hurried on his way by Nellie's strenuous efforts during the storm.

After those meetings, Nellie and I returned to Emmanuel Missionary College so I could finish my education. It was while we were living there that we had Ronald, our second son. He was born on February 6, 1942, in the home of Dr. Robert Boothby. That dear doctor lived near the college and was a true friend of students, to be sure. He kept his obstetrical fees to the minimum, to say the least—in fact, just $35.00!

Our third son was a Washington Sanitarium

product—born on July 19, 1949, in the hospital near the General Conference offices where I worked in the Ministerial Association. Bob was a lovable son from the very beginning. Nellie and I were deeply thankful for our three healthy, active young sons.

But the Lord's plan evidently was to break the "son cycle" and give us a daughter the next time around. It happened after we moved to Glendale, California, to spend a year following up telecast interests. We were hoping for a daughter, of course. Well, Dr. Bruce Brown said that the heartbeat was slow, which suggested to him another boy. As a result, we had no name for our baby that happy day, April 25, 1956, when she arrived at the Glendale Adventist Hospital. The boys took the matter in hand and named her "Connie Jean." Fortunately, she has always been satisfied with their choice. The joy of this very young lady joining the Vandeman family was not even muted by the fact that Nellie's arms were covered with poison ivy at the time of birth, so she couldn't hold the baby for two full weeks. In fact, when word reached our head office in Washington, D.C., Roy Anderson, my chief, and the secretaries danced around his desk at the news of the Vandeman baby *girl*.

And now we must look to the passing years. This section of our story might well be called "Triumph and Tragedy." Maybe that's overstated. There's been, however, a lot of triumph and some deep concerns. There have been shadows within the family circle. Times of sadness and anxious concern. But God has never failed us.

In 1969 our third son, Bob, was drafted and sent to Vietnam. While he served halfway around the world, we wrote regularly, of course, and eagerly anticipated his letters back to us. Occasionally we were even able to get a phone call through or make a connection via shortwave radio. These were always treasured times that cheered us all and gave Bob the assurance that he was loved and supported at home.

But one Saturday evening, a uniformed officer rang our front doorbell and soberly proffered a black-bordered envelope. We hadn't experienced this before and immediately feared the worst. Our hearts were in our throats. We soon gratefully learned, however, that it wasn't just death notices that were delivered to parents' homes in this manner. The same ominous envelope carried notices of other less catastrophic casualties. After we'd quickly opened the telegram, our eyes raced to these words in the middle of a paragraph: "Not seriously wounded—we repeat, not seriously wounded." What a relief. Thanksgiving and gratitude swept over the family.

A few days later, we were astounded to hear Bob himself on the phone. "Dad and Mom," he said, "I've been shipped home to Walter Reed Hospital in my pajamas." I'm sure we exceeded the speed limit that day as we drove the ten miles to that grand old institution, Walter Reed Hospital. How could we be so fortunate when so many families didn't fare as well?

In recent years, our deepest and most lingering concerns have centered on our son Ronald. Ron was a young man of exceptional ability and promise. He proved to be an excellent speaker. In his senior year at his academy (high school) he won the areawide Temperance Oratorical Contest. And, even now, he is asked by the Mental Health staff on special occasions to give readings for the entertainment of the other clients, as other patients are called. But in his late teens and early twenties, he developed a serious mental illness. After his second year of college in California, he had a complete breakdown. He was working for a friend of ours. Of course, I flew out there to be by his side as quickly as possible and brought him back home.

For more than thirty years, we have prayed and fasted, studied the problem, consulted experts, searched everywhere for answers—always watching intently for some hopeful signs of improvement. Parents who have gone through this kind of tragedy will understand our experience during these intervening years more than others.

As we checked out various facilities along the East Coast and in Canada, we met many skilled and caring physicians, among them Dr. George Harding, Sr., of Worthington, Ohio; Dr. Abram Hoffer of Saskatoon, Canada; and Dr. Humphrey Osmond of Princeton University Medical Center. It was Dr. Osmond who said, "I'm amazed at the way this young man handles himself, as sick as he is. The only explanation for this is that he is extremely intelligent, has great insight into his

49

illness, and is fighting a courageous battle against it."

When we moved west in the autumn of 1971, Ron came with us to the Los Angeles area. He is now in a most helpful board-and-care facility within a few miles of our home. This makes it easier for us to give him all the time and attention he can absorb. Ron has always been quite sensitive spiritually. He still refers to the time when he gave his heart to Jesus and talks occasionally about traveling with Dad. Ron always liked to go to meetings where he could sit in the back and sing his heart out. Nellie and I are confident that he will be among the saved.

I have to say a word about the time when Ron attempted to take my life, because it has been so widely publicized. It's important to put that crucial moment in perspective. Ron was living with us at the time. His physician had withdrawn his regular medication for a few weeks and replaced it with another. Ron and I were walking toward the car parked in our driveway when he suddenly reacted dramatically to the chemical changes in his body and lashed out at me from behind with a kitchen knife.

But Providence intervened. Harold Reiner, one of my associates, lived only a block away. He went out just at that time to pick up some computer parts. As he was driving by, he took in the situation at a glance. Harold jumped out and shouted to Ron. Ron stopped his attack immediately and became calm—as if something had snapped back into place inside him. As it turned out, Harold had come by in the nick of time. The doctor later reported that if it had been fifteen seconds later, he would have been too late.

After the incident, the authorities had to arrest Ron and bring charges against him. When I saw him for the first time two weeks later, he said, "Please forgive me, Dad. I'm so sorry. I didn't know what I was doing." We are thankful that the judge handed out no punitive sentence but simply gave instruction for his care, care that continues to this day. One newspaper described the incident as a "no-fault tragedy." Nellie and I deeply appreciate the prayers that have been offered for Ron and for ourselves concerning this matter. Thank you again and again. A photograph of Ron at thirteen years of age appears in the picture section of this book.

What about the rest of the "younger Vandemans"? What are they doing now? Well, as you would expect, only one of them has changed *her* name. Connie is now Connie Jeffery. She met her husband, Ron Jeffery, while in England attending Newbold College. They have been married seventeen years and have an adorable ten-year-old son, Craig. Ron has been a wonderful father and remains a very pleasant and fun part of our family.

And what do you know, the Jefferys now live just five minutes from Nellie and me. We feel extremely fortunate. Craig can skateboard or rollerblade to our home in a matter of minutes. You can imagine how welcome he is day or night.

Our son Bob has chosen the southland for his home—the only member of the family who lives far away from us. He is doing very well in the automobile business in Atlanta. Georgia has been his home for many years, and he has acquired a southern accent, as has his daughter, Holli. She is now studying court reporting. Holli is a carbon copy of her mother, Nancy.

That leaves our eldest, George. George has always been a warm-hearted, family-oriented father and now is a grandfather himself, at fifty-five years of age. That makes Nellie and me the proud *great*-grandparents of little Jeremy John, the child of George's daughter, Shelli, and her husband, Duane. And what a treasure Jeremy is! Please see his picture in his great-grandfather's arms in the picture section. Our family gatherings sometimes number from ten to fourteen; when friends join us, the group can swell to twenty. This is now too much for us to handle. So we have most of our family gatherings at the home of George and his sweet little wife, Wini. What special and happy events these are—holidays, birthdays, etc.

George has been an attorney of note, one of the three senior partners of the international law firm Latham & Watkins, headquartered here in Los Angeles. In the picture section of this book, you will see a full-page *Newsweek* photo that shows George walking briskly down a New York sidewalk with one of his clients, Ted Turner, the owner of the Turner Broadcasting System and CNN.

The Vandeman family circle has always been

happy and lively in spite of the shadows that have come to us.

After the children were grown and gone from the home nest, Nellie took a more active part with me in the television outreach. Evidently the *difference* in our personalities brought a special interest and excitement to our ministry team.

For instance, at one large camp meeting, the conference president leaned over to Nellie after she had spoken and whispered, "You humanize the guy." *I wonder what he meant!* At another large rally at the Sligo Church in Takoma Park, Maryland, I had started to tell a story, hesitated, and then started again to tell the story, changed my mind, and said, "Nellie, you can really tell it better than I can."

She leaned over to the microphone and said, "Faster, for sure."

Interestingly enough, at the tribute held for my retirement, one of our dear friends, Dr. Joan Coggin of the Loma Linda Heart Team, was asked to emcee the occasion. Those who have known her will spontaneously chuckle when her name is mentioned. Joan is a sought-after speaker and entertainer. She has the gift of intermingling spiritual gems with her humor. That night, Dr. Coggin talked about my dependence on Nellie when it comes to remembering names. It was choice, so I will quote her word for word.

George will forget someone's name, and the first thing he does is start searching

for Nellie, who has never forgotten a name
in her whole life. If you ever want to see
a fearful sight, have Nellie be out of the
room, and George is smiling as the
person is approaching him. But you look
in his eyes; it's that cornered look that
the wild animal gets when you shine a
beam of light, you know. He is smiling,
and total panic is in the eyes. And I've
been standing nearby, and he's turned
to me, and I've said, "I don't know. I don't
know!" You don't need to say the words;
you know what the problem is. And that's
real anguish.

But then, if Nellie is in the vicinity, this
fascinating little game takes place. You see,
first of all, Nellie sees Fred and Susan
Smith approaching, and she says in
George's hearing, "Oh, look dear, here
come Fred and Susan Smith." It sort of
reminds me of when you went to see Santa
Claus. And you couldn't figure out how
Santa knew your name. And as you would
walk down to Santa, a person would say
in the hidden microphone, "Go right ahead,
Joan. Santa is waiting." And when you get
there, Santa says, "Hello, Joan." How does
he know my name? Well, Fred and Susan
Smith had that same relationship with the
Vandemans.

Or there is another little thing where he
thinks she is in the vicinity, but he can't
spot her, and so he sort of issues this crying

call, "Nellie, look who's here!" Which is translated, "Nellie, *who* are these lovely people?"

Our daughter Connie has a genuine interest in *It Is Written*. She has done a lot of singing for the program. And what a sense of humor she has. Connie has said she intends to keep all the humorous outtakes from the videotaping sessions of our program and vows someday to reveal them to the amusement and "embarrassment" of her dad.

One of these experiences took place when we taped the program "How to Live With a Tiger." When the real tiger was brought into the studio, a lot of hasty maneuvering took place that never appeared on television. The young tiger really had no interest in hurting me; he was just in an energetic mood. But he grabbed the arm of my leather chair in his powerful jaws and hurled it across the studio, knocking me over in the process. No harm was intended—just a playful prank.

I shall always be able to point out those teeth marks on our studio furniture. But Connie wants more of a memorial—the videotape of the entire action as the cameras continued to roll.

On another occasion, I was discussing the discord between capital and labor described in James 5 as one of the conditions of the end times. That day, I had on an exceptionally worn-out pair of shoes—layer after layer of worn leather—you could almost see the socks.

You see, the camera shots never include my feet. So, during the long hours of taping in the studio, I can wear my oldest pair of shoes; they are *so* comfortable.

Well, during one break between the "takes," the director began talking to me about the script as the makeup woman was touching up my face. I sat on the set in my leather chair with my legs crossed. Evidently, my left foot swung up in front of a camera nearby. That cameraman decided to get a closeup, zooming in until my pathetically worn shoe filled most of the screen. Control booth personnel then proceeded to superimpose the text from James 5 over this shoe.

When we were all ready to resume our taping, the director asked me to turn and look at the monitor to preview some "special footage." And there, moving slowly up the screen so they could be read easily, were the words of James 5:1-3, superimposed on my ragged shoe: "Go to now, ye rich men, weep and howl for your miseries that shall come upon you. Your riches are corrupted, and your garments are motheaten. Your gold and silver is cankered; and the rust of them shall be a witness against you." Well, you can imagine the studio erupting into good-natured laughter and myself, of course, joining with them. And, you guessed it, Connie wants the event kept on record.

Knowing this, you won't be surprised at this tongue-in-cheek letter Connie sent me after her freshman year in college as an English major.

26 July 1974URGENT MEMORANDUM
George Edward Vandeman
Dearest Father:

In my proofreading of several of your letters while you were away, I have noticed something quite peculiar. You seem to have an obsession with the word MUCH! Following are only a few of the phrases that you use with exceedingly excessive repetition:

Thank-you MUCH
The Lord bless you MUCH
I have been traveling MUCH
God has blessed us MUCH
May He bless you MUCH

It would seem that a man of your extraordinary and unique intelligence would utilize much more innovative and creative and fresh words in expressing himself than the rather trite MUCH, don't you think? This, however, is only a suggestion to a man of your experience and intelligence. If you are, by any chance, interested to know how I would revise your phrases befitting to a man of your caliber, please don't hesitate to contact me any time of the day or night. This issue is too vitally important to wait MUCH longer.

Pending proof to the contrary, I shall remain humbly,

Ms. Connie Jean Vandeman
Chairman of the Committee to make IIW

the number-one television program in the whole world.

OK, Connie, I have very MUCH learned my lesson!

This chapter on the Vandeman family would not be complete without the fascinating story of our trip to Hunza—the Shangri-la of the Himalayas, the place where so many people live past the age of one hundred. Our son George had happily agreed to send our three grandchildren, Shelli, Brad, and Craig, with their mother, Judy. He knew that I wanted this to be a people-to-people project. So watch out for "exaggeration," because it's Grandpa and Grandma who are telling the story. Here is Nellie's introduction to the event.

For twenty-five years George had had a dream of taking a trip to Hunza, the tiny country nestled high in the Himalayan Mountains in the Pakistan-controlled part of Kajhmir near the borders of China and Afghanistan. He had heard about this country and of the lives of the Hunza people, many of whom remain strong and active even at well over a hundred years. He had read about their simple diet, mainly fruits, grains, and vegetables, and their lives, which include much vigorous exercise. It was hard to imagine that there was a country where the people were living in complete peace, free from the major fears of humankind—disease and war. Surely, he thought, they have something to offer the world. He had an insatiable desire and dream to visit this little country someday.

Yes, we had corresponded with the king, or the mir, as he is called, and cleared all travel arrangements and were ready to go—camera crew and all. I hoped that I'd have the opportunity to talk personally with the mir—the forty-year-old monarch who speaks English fluently. Within minutes, long-distance information revealed the number of the palace in Karinabad, capital of Hunza. There was only one phone number listed, with the obvious number "*one*."

When I placed a call, the mir answered the phone personally. I found him most cordial and anxious for our arrival. I asked if there was anything he might wish me to bring. "Yes, please, a pair of *designer jeans*." I asked about his size, etc. Then he asked if we could bring a "cardigan" for his wife. Well, *cardigan* is a good British word for a sweater. I asked for her size. "Oh, she's a little thing," he replied. We settled the matter by deciding to bring several sizes for the royal family to choose from.

Now a secret. You may already know that Nellie doesn't enjoy flying and that her fear of airplanes has grown through the years. Nellie had heard that the trip from Rawalpindi, Pakistan, to Gilgit, the last outpost before Hunza, would be a hazardous flight between the narrow confines of a deep gorge, with towering Himalayan peaks on either side. After boarding the plane, she learned, furthermore, that the route was so narrow that the plane would not be able to turn around if we encountered any difficulties.

We survived the flight into Gilgit just fine, but the road from there into Hunza gave us a few thrills of its own. It is built into the cliffs and mountainsides of the Himalayas. Fortunately, it had just been rebuilt and proved to be very wide, well paved, and safe. In the distance we could see the old roadway—hanging perilously, it seemed, from sheer cliffs. The stories of travel on that old road would take a full chapter to describe. I was told that nearly five hundred workers lost their lives in building the new road.

During our stay in Hunza, Nellie made a delightful and enthusiastic hostess for our team. She loved the rani—that is the title for the lovely queen—and their children. Shelli, Brad, and Craig had brought along frisbees and other toys with which to entertain the children. They all became inseparable during the time we were there.

Our breakfasts were served in the three guest homes; we ate the other meals in the elegant palace dining room. We had so many choices that there was little difficulty in meeting our needs.

But here is one on me. One day we were taping a segment for the television program. All the family stood at the edge of a precipice looking down at the raging Hunza River below. I was beginning a story and made a number of "false starts" before the camera. I always try to make certain that the first words of a segment sound natural and direct. But on that day, I had to try again and again, four, eight, twelve, seventeen times, before we got the segment down without mistakes. And what a price I had to pay! Nellie, Judy, and my grandchildren have never let me live that one down.

But thank God, we accomplished what we had come to Hunza for—an official appearance of the mir at the palace in ceremonial dress. That interview was priceless. The whole story of Hunza emerged in living detail. It started with some deserters from the army of Alexander the Great who escaped into the Hunza Valley, never to be apprehended. These became the founders of the Hunza people. And these people, in turn, have taught the outside world something important about healthful living.

An Australian diplomat to Pakistan and Hunza was present with us, along with his lovely wife. He confided that he had been raised on Wheetabix, a product of the successful Adventist health food company in Australia. We began a lasting friendship.

We also taped segments with ordinary people in Hunza and conducted home interviews in which Nellie participated in the lives of the people; she particularly enjoyed learning about their cooking habits.

The last scene I remember took place at the palace. I can still picture it: the rani hugging Nellie and our guests and everyone, especially the children, expressing their love and appreciation for each other. Among those saying goodbye was a tall youth named Amjed, an admirer of sixteen-year-old Shelli, our granddaughter. He wrote her a beautiful letter a few weeks later, saying:

> "Some people make heart in your home
> and you cannot forget them forever."

Yes, the Hunza experience was a choice assignment the Vandemans will never forget.

Four

"The Bible Is the Star of This Show!"

God's providential working in the start of our *It Is Written* ministry is the part of this story that I most enjoy reliving. How was *It Is Written* born? Let me take you through the crucial early stages one by one.

I'm not sure whose idea it was, but early on in my ministry at the General Conference, I was asked to travel with my family to London, England, and spend a full year sharing the gospel in that great city. Now, London, as you know, is a huge metropolis. But its great size lies in its expanse—not in its height. In the 1950s, no London building stood higher than six stories, and yet the number of its residents exceeded the population of the three Scandinavian countries put together.

Our daughter, Connie, was, at the time, only a sparkle in our eyes. We took our three boys and boarded the *Queen Mary* with a small mountain of luggage—boxes and boxes of books for our outreach in London, plus the special foods we felt our family might need. In 1952, England was still rationing butter and orange juice. There was also a limited supply of milk—something that our small Bobby needed regularly.

We found beautiful people in England and formed lasting friendships. One of them came as a happy surprise. Dr. Jim Schooley; "Mim," his sweet wife; and their two children had arrived in England, where Jim served as a medical officer in the armed forces. Our two families spent a lot of time together during the first months of our time there. We will always remember Dr. Schooley taking us to the PX for root-beer floats. Can you imagine how refreshing they tasted in that faraway land?

But now down to business. I was scheduled to conduct meetings in London's Coliseum Theater. There were three tiers of circular balconies above the main floor. This historic building, adjacent to Trafalgar Square, seated two thousand people. The stout little manager couldn't understand why we were paying for this theater for religious meetings. He was certain no one would attend.

He was greatly surprised later when we asked to reserve the theater for two, and later three, sessions on a single Sunday. God did something special that year in London. We found that even three sessions were not enough to hold the crowds who came out. Several thousand were turned away. We discovered that people were actually standing in line, four deep, four blocks long, before the meetings were scheduled to open. (You can see a picture of the crowds in the photo section.) A few scuffles even broke out among people seeking a place in line, and ambulances had to be summoned. The neighboring liquor store even threatened to sue the theater for loss of business that day. When the doors were opened, people were almost trampled; the police were called and, of course, that brought in the press.

Well, you can imagine how the British press in the 1950s would treat an American causing such a disturbance! One of the reporters for the *London Express* told me after the three sessions that I would be a success in my meetings because an actor on that same stage had been a dismal failure *until* he fell and broke his nose in front of the entrance. The publicity brought him the crowds he needed to survive. *How encouraging!*

Then a tabloid newspaper put a picture of Nellie and me on its front page with the caption: "Vandeman has a telephone—six hundred thousand Britishers can't get one." (Post-war shortages, no doubt.) George and Nellie Vandeman were learning fast.

Aside from all the commotion, the meetings were a wonderful inspiration. Ben Glanzer, from the United States, led the splendid choir. My first topic, "The Heavens Are Telling," showed how the wonders of astronomy revealed a Creator. Little did I dream that this subject would capture British attention. But it did—one woman climbed the three floors to the top balcony, only to be turned away by the ushers; every seat was filled. She cried, "And all I wanted was a *look up.*" The people of Britain were weary and hungry for encouragement and truth.

We shall always love these wonderful people. We will never forget the precious individuals and families who discovered the truth in Jesus Christ during that time.

At the end of that year, just when our boys were becoming a little weary of England and hoping to travel back to the United States, the leadership of the church asked me to stay a second year. They promised to finance the purchase of a suitable auditorium for an evangelistic center in that city. The boys and Nellie were good sports, and we stayed.

This was at the time of the coronation of Queen Elizabeth. You really have to live through a British coronation to believe the splendor, pomp, and ceremony. There was a light drizzle that day. The boys went with family friends and the woman who often took care of Bobby and stood for several hours watching the event from the sidewalk. But Nellie and I were "chicken," I suppose, and rented a "telly," as they call it, to watch the festivities in the warmth and quiet of our home.

I must say that I also enjoyed the experience of searching for a permanent center for evangelism in London—with something like a blank check in my pocket to pay for it. Let me explain.

For many years, the General Conference had been saving their yearly allotment for the China Division budget. Finally, since there seemed to be little hope of the work in Communist China opening again for years to come, they voted to spend that nest egg—over one and one quarter million dollars—on evangelistic centers in New York City, Chicago, and London. That's where the money came from.

What happened in London reminds me of God's promise: "Before they call, I will answer" (Isaiah 65:24). We discovered that the New Gallery Center at 123 Regent Street, of all places, was available for us to purchase. It was a magnificent theater. The land actually belonged to the queen. In fact, she owned the entire street under all these great buildings. But the New Gallery Center itself belonged to J. Arthur Rank, the British philanthropist and movie maker. He sold it us for fifty thousand British pounds. The exchange at that time was five dollars to one pound, so we ended up purchasing the building for $250,000. This left us more than sufficient funds to remodel the theater. The building provided us with a beautiful auditorium, offices, a reading room, a second auditorium in the large basement, and a canteen which we turned into a health-food restaurant. A government post office was tucked into the building on the side street.

In those post-war years, some anti-American sentiment was quite evident. But that changed—radically changed—not only among the reporters but among the city officials as well. The New Gallery began to offer inspiring music concerts for the public every noon and health classes of all kinds for the store clerks and the public on Regent Street. More and more people began to open their hearts to our evangelistic team and to the church. So much so that Prince Philip sent me a letter of appreciation for our community work in the heart of the west end of London. I knew we'd been accepted when I received an invitation to join the conservative Westminster Chamber of Commerce.

All this was a splendid testimony to the influence of Bible truth and Christian kindness from our people in the heart of the west end of London. I will always remember the humbling and awesome sensation of standing in that pulpit in the heart of the city of John and Charles Wesley and George Whitefield, three evangelical giants of the eighteenth century. Two hundred years after them, I found myself still carrying on the work of helping to transform men and women with the gospel of Jesus Christ. What an honor!

Most important of all, we also built, in the New Gallery, a well-equipped baptistery. It was set in front of the huge theater organ and was used *again* and *again* and *again* to the glory of God. That blessed payoff is what we shall long remember.

"Long remember," yes. But we left behind a treasure—a little baby boy who succumbed in a premature birth. Nellie came through this not without a struggle—but finally OK with the help of Dr. Schooley and our local physician friends. For that we are very grateful. We named the little fellow Philip Charles after the royal family. My three boys found some measure of comfort when I took them to the funeral home to see their tiny, perfectly formed brother and spoke of us meeting him again in heaven. Little Philip Charles, however, did leave us a tie to London that will never be broken.

Back in the United States, we found that a new venture in ministry awaited us. Some years earlier, a Southern California Conference worker named Torel Seat—a man ahead of his time in many ways—had made a series of black-and-white sixteen-milimeter film sermons for home Bible study. This was before television really got a foothold in the American population. Torel Seat, H. M. S. Richards, and I had preached our favorite evangelistic sermons for this series, which was filmed in the old Hal Roach Studios. We were provided with a backdrop, a plain pulpit, and a few flowers in front of the pulpit. Our Bible and sermon notes were our responsibility.

It was remarkable the way our church people responded to these Bible studies on film. Nothing like this had been available before. As primitive as those programs were by contemporary standards, they were sold widely in the United States and overseas.

Several years later, after television had grown more popular, an Adventist businessman by the name of Paul James, along with his Roman Catholic partner, planned to put these films on television in Midland, Texas. TV was all black and white back then. A dear friend of mine, Dick Baron, was the pastor there. He was young and innovative. He took those films—some thirty, some forty, some fifty minutes long—and edited them into one-hour programs, adding musical numbers with his splendid singing voice.

Paul James's daughter, Pauline, then only twelve years old, will never forget that experience. Providentially, she is now one of our valuable workers at the It Is Written office in Thousand Oaks, California. She is the wife of our Pacific Union Conference president, Thomas Mostert. We were talking about the old days as I was preparing this chapter, and she told me that their family was the only one that owned a television set in their seventy-member church. So each Sunday, between thirty and fifty of these faithful people met at their home to see the program. Pauline's mother prepared delightful food each week to grace the occasion.

Perhaps those under sixty-five who are reading these pages may not remember how rare TV sets were then in the average home. Even as late as 1956, when we aired the program in Washington, D.C., so few members had sets that many came to the Sligo Adventist Church and viewed the program there. F. D. Nichol, our respected *Review and Herald* editor, came to view with other members.

I will never forget the day the General Conference president, James L. McElhany, called me into his office to talk about "the future." He leaned toward me and whispered softly, "Mrs. McElhany and I have a television set at home." Then I leaned over the desk and whispered, "We do too."

So remarkable was the response from the population of Midland, Texas, and the surrounding country that church leaders began to see the possibility of a *full-message* television program.

Shortly after I returned from London, they sent me to hold reaping meetings in Midland. The result was actually the beginning of the *It Is Written* program. I saw the enormous potential of linking television broadcasts with personal evangelistic effort—visiting the homes of interested individuals there in the city who had watched our program. One day, we visited the home of a banker. Sitting there on his sofa, he pointed to his TV set and said, "That is where I learned to study the Bible. Thank you so much for coming into this living room and meeting our needs."

After the Midland experience, we were ready for stage two. About that time, the Faith for Today ministry was filming a drama program in New York City featuring Pastor William Fagal. This farseeing pioneer was carrying on a splendid work with little support. Church leaders decided that we could supplement this drama outreach with a full-message approach. So they sent me to California to produce a sample.

A woman named Penny Edwards and her husband, Ralph, were commissioned to produce this pilot program. She was an actress who had joined the church along with her husband, a Hollywood casting director. It was Penny Edwards who came up with the name "It Is Written." We shall always love her for that. Some at the time had their doubts about "It Is Written" being a suitable title for something on television. But others of us believed that the phrase fit what we wanted to express through television so perfectly. And in our discussions we referred to the title of what was then a new TV show called *I Love Lucy.* These days, that program has become familiar all over the world. But back then, the phrase seemed more than a little odd for a TV program. But it soon became a hit. We believed that our title was as appealing as Lucy's in its own way. And I think time has confirmed that conviction.

The first program, unfortunately, was not too successful. In fact, I was never shown the film produced in that initial effort. Our director, Ralph Edwards, being from a Hollywood background, tried to make an actor out of me, and of course, he failed. I'm no dramatist; what I do best is to speak to the viewer heart to heart. And that connection just can't be choreographed.

After a long sequence of events, I found myself in New York City filming *It Is Written* in the Charter Oak Studios on 94th Street, where *Faith for Today* was also produced. Three talented brothers produced our program quite professionally. Believe it or not, at that time *Faith for Today* and *It Is Written* were the only regular religious programs on the airwaves across the United States—except for Oral Roberts and Bishop Sheen. What an opportunity!

One day during a lunch break in our television shooting at Charter Oak, a visitor happened to pass through the semidarkened studio and asked, "What is this show all about?" Our Roman Catholic director immediately responded, "The *Bible* is the star of this show." He understood, didn't he? I'm so happy that same "star" has remained at the center of *It Is Written* to this day.

Five

Growth Beyond Our Wildest Dreams

How could I begin so important a chapter as this one? Believe me, I spent a lot of time trying to decide. You see, information such as this chapter contains, coming from me personally, could easily be misunderstood. The truth is, while I shall be eternally grateful for what has been accomplished through the It Is Written ministry, I realize very well it is *our Lord* who deserves *all* the credit.

Keeping that great truth in mind, let me venture to state that because of the wide reach of television, George Vandeman has been heard and seen by more people than any other Adventist minister in our history. In recent years the *It Is Written* telecast has been viewed each week by some twenty-five million people around the world.

It is difficult to really understand these figures—twenty-five million people weekly, multiplied by fifty-two weeks, leads us to the staggering total of one billion, three hundred million. Of course, many of the same people watch throughout the year. But remember, this total number is for only one year, not three or four. You can see that the actual total multiyear result is staggering. God has used and is using the awesome power of television to reach an incredible number of people, millions of hearts and minds.

We thank God for these viewers—people who recognize me just about everywhere I go, even to this day. Please don't misunderstand. This doesn't make me a celebrity; it just shows how widely our message is being spread. I meet viewers on airplanes, in shopping malls, on the streets of large and small cities, and overseas as well. The earliest indication of this came during a fiftieth-anniversary trip Nellie and I took to China. Our son, George, Jr., arranged for this trip as an anniversary present. We traveled on the splendid Singapore World Airways. Knowing we are not accustomed to first-class travel, George arranged just that for us. As we stepped into the first-class area, the flight attendant stopped me and exclaimed, "Pastor Vandeman, I watch you every Sunday that I'm home in Rome, Italy."

Now the fact that strangers sometimes recognize me is not that important. But I do acknowledge encounters like that one as a sure sign that television carries the warmth of personal contact for Christ everywhere the airwaves flash. Please notice what Ellen White said: "So abundantly will the renewing Spirit of God have crowned with success the intensely active agencies, that the light of present truth will be seen flashing everywhere" *(Evangelism,* 694).

You will forgive me for thinking that God gave Ellen White this unusual insight because He could foresee what television would accomplish. This nineteenth-century religious leader could not have known personally that television signals would someday flash around the world like "jets of light. But she saw a vision of "jets of light shining from cities and villages until "God's Word was obeyed, and as a result there were memorials for Him in *every town and village*" (*Evangelism,* 699).

But now back to earth! Let me take you back to the remarkable statement that the manager of Soviet national television made to me: "*I am asking you to be the moral voice for my country.*" I'd like to explain how the very meaningful visit with this man came about.

The story really begins in the summer of 1990 during the General Conference session of the Adventist Church held in Indianapolis, Indiana. It was there that Nellie and I met Elena and Natasha. Elena was actually the "Barbara Walters" of Russian television. Natasha was her translator. They were attending the General Conference session, at the invitation of the Russian Adventist delegation, to film a story on the

Adventist Church. As Nellie and I spent time with these two people, we developed a very precious bond of friendship. And later, Elena and Natasha began to lay the groundwork for Soviet national television to accept us on those nationwide airwaves.

They had been working at Soviet national television headquarters in Moscow for some time. And Elena was sure the time had come for television exposure for the Adventist Church in Russia. So she invited me to come to Moscow to appear on the popular prime-time program *Good Evening Moscow*. I did so and received the warmest welcome from the master of ceremonies and his staff. What seemed so remarkable was that this warmth was actually taking place within the walls of the network through which Communism was making its last frantic attempt to control the minds of the people.

But isn't that the way God works?

We made other visits to that "stronghold." In fact, our contacts became so routine and comfortable that finally I was welcomed in a special way by the general manager himself and invited to become the "moral voice" for his country.

After this thrilling development, our own dear Peter Kulakov, the speaker for *Voice of Hope* and manager of the Voice of Hope Media Center, became the key to getting us a substantial television release that would reach the millions spread throughout the former Soviet Union.

Our Russian friends, Elena and Natasha, even played a key role in dramatically expanding our television coverage in the United States. Here's how it happened.

One year, we were able to arrange for Elena and Natasha to attend with us the Religion in Media awards banquet at the Beverly Wilshire Hotel in Hollywood. That's where six hundred to eight hundred leading producers and TV personalities representing various religious groups meet annually to receive silver and gold Angel Awards for excellence in media. The "Angels" are something like the Emmys awarded once a year to secular television directors, actors, etc.

Mary Dorr, founder of Religion in Media, has been a good friend to It Is Written. She agreed that it would be appropriate for us to present the Russian women with a silver Angel Award that night. It was a stirring moment. The audience sat in almost reverent silence as I told the story of Elena, the "Barbara Walters" of Russia. Then Elena spoke, and Natasha translated. Afterward, they received the award amid enthusiastic applause. (There is a picture of them, along with Mary Dorr; actress Donna Douglas, who was in charge; and myself in the picture pages of this book.)

That night, Paul Crouch and his wife, Jan, the owners of Trinity Broadcasting System, were sitting in the audience. Their conservative religious network has built up a staggering audience in the United States and overseas. They had received several Angel Awards that night as well. The next Monday morning, we received a phone call from Paul Crouch at the It Is Written offices. He told us how impressed he was with Elena and Natasha. And then, to my great surprise and joy, he offered to place *It Is Written* in a choice Sunday-morning telecast hour on his network for only *one-half the regular price.* We were stunned and deeply grateful.

In the years since then, our records show that the response from his immense audience has been the largest we receive from any network we're privileged to use. *Praise God for this!*

But now back to Russia. Peter Kulakov is really the one who, under the blessing of God, secured prime evening time to release our program to be broadcast throughout Russia. In fact, *It Is Written* was aired during the best of prime time: 6:30 Monday evenings. What gave him influence with the television industry in Russia was his officially granted license to operate in the field of radio and television—the only nongovernment Russian at the time with such authority.

But during the weeks and months of negotiation that followed, we encountered many complications and roadblocks. Telephone connections with Russia were spotty and exasperatingly slow and tedious. Sometimes we would have to wait for hours to get through, sometimes days. This was during the chaotic time when political power was transferred from the purely Communist system to the Yeltsin regime. Today, it's much easier to make contacts.

During recent years, we've enjoyed wonderful television coverage in Russia. Pastor Mark Finley has stepped into the role of *It Is Written* speaker and has seen providence after providence turn the tide of national chaos into sweeping victory for the cause of Christ. First, he conducted very successful evangelistic meetings in Moscow's Plekhanov Hall. Then he had the incredible opportunity to hold meetings in the Congress Hall of the Kremlin itself. To do justice to what happened there is far beyond the scope of this volume. Suffice it to say that God continued to bless.

We saw history in the making as Mark was able to preach an evangelistic series in Moscow's huge Olympic Stadium. It was my privilege to assist Mark in this effort. Since, up to that time, I had been the principle *It Is Written* speaker in Russia and had established a presence, it was thought best for me to travel to Moscow and link up with Mark in proclaiming the gospel to the citizens of that great city. Thousands had already been converted and baptized through Mark's Plekhanov and Kremlin meetings. I worked with him during the first four nights at the Olympic Stadium, speaking for four or five minutes before Mark's main presentation. I will never forget the Russian people's wonderfully warm response.

You may have heard that Mark faced some noisy and violent opposition during those first few nights. A fanatical cult was determined to disrupt our gospel presentations. On more than one occasion, several individuals of this radical element rushed to the stage and attacked Mark in order to get access to the microphone. The huge stage was about five feet above the floor of the stadium. A series of steps, thirty-feet wide, were built to accommodate the large choirs that sang night after night. It was up these steps that the agitators ran—all at once, as if on cue. Sitting only eight feet behind Mark, I watched them come. Fortunately, our very able bodied ushers came to the rescue and managed to stop these people just in time. But I also noticed that Mark was able to proceed calmly and coolly in spite of this terrible provocation. I could imagine a mighty angel standing by his side. Mark responded graciously. You can imagine how this won the audience to his side. They were furious at those trying to disrupt the meeting, and their loud applause when these people were taken out of the stadium strengthened Mark's hands.

During Mark's earlier meetings, a former KGB officer named Boris and three other former KGB men accepted Christ and were baptized. These were among the able men who sprang to their feet, intervened, and saved the day. Boris himself tackled one troublemaker and in an instant had him pinned to the floor of the stage (I actually heard his head thud against it). Boris's expert training as a KGB agent came in very handy on behalf of a gospel crusade! From the time of the first disturbance, Boris and his men stayed by Mark's side every moment he was in the Olympic Stadium. It was an inspiration to see.

The results of Mark's Moscow experience are unforgettable. Before these meetings began, there was one Adventist church in Moscow, with seven hundred members. There are now twelve churches in the city with a membership of four

The Family

George and Nellie Vandeman on their wedding day, October 2, 1938.

Can you recognize George in this early family photo?

George at 14.

George's parents, Herbert and Nina Vandeman.

Nellie's parents, Sverre and Inga Johnson.

Nellie and her three boys in 1950.

Nellie and the boys—ready for overseas assignment.

A visit to Holland.

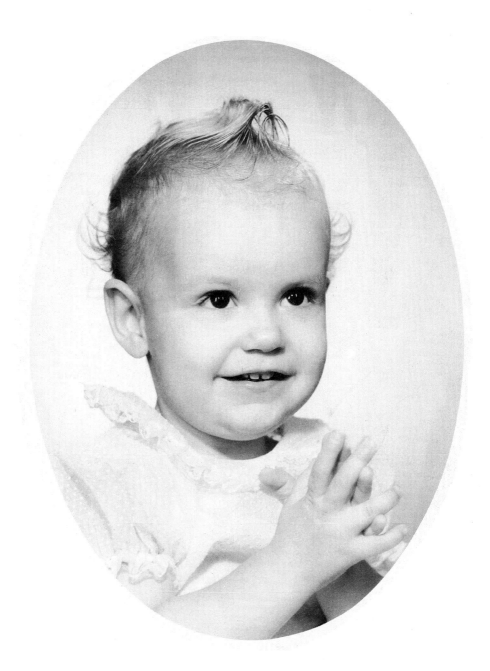

George and Nellie's only daughter, Connie.

Attorney George Vandeman, Jr., with his client Ted Turner of Turner Broadcasting and CNN (courtesy *Newsweek*, photo by Robert Moss).

Ronald at 13.

Bob in his military uniform.

Son Bob especially enjoyed horses as a boy.

The next generations

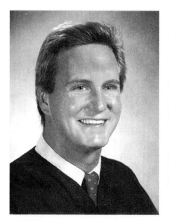

Brad Vandeman, son of
George, Jr.

Shelli Kozachenko, daughter
of George, Jr., and mother of
great-grandson Jeremy.

Craig Vandeman, youngest
son of George, Jr.

Holli Vandeman, daughter
of Bob.

Connie's son Craig enthusiastically
teaching Grandpa his computer technique.

Proud great-grandfather
with Shelli's son, Jeremy.

The Ministry

Getting started in radio.

The stage during the evangelistic series at the London Coliseum Theater (see chapter 4).

The theater was "full to the rafters" three times in one day.

At the Dead Sea caves.

At ancient Tyre.

With the mir and rani of Hunza.

Sharing the *It Is Written* set with a tiger.

Out to lunch?

In 1979, Andrews University awarded
George a Doctor of Divinity degree.

Famous Acquaintances

Some of the world's greatest people with whom George Vandeman had significant personal relationships.

Meeting Paul Harvey in 1962.

Grandson Craig on Paul Harvey's lap.

With President Gerald Ford in the Oval Office.

Lowell Thomas, who asked *It Is Written* to operate the Spafford orphanage (courtesy CBS News Photo).

J. C. Penney (courtesy JCPenney Corporation).

With archaeologist Yigael Yadin (center) in Israel (photo courtesy of Institute of Archaeology, Andrews University).

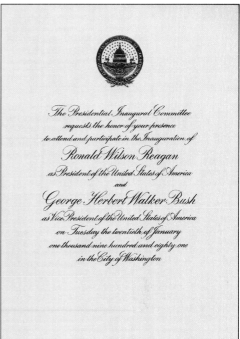

Two of the three Presidents George knew best.

A very special invitation.

With Donna Douglas, Elena, the Barbara Walters of Russia, her translator, Natasha, and Mary Dorr, of Religion in Media Awards.

The Vandemans and Finleys with the technical staff who produce *It Is Written*.

thousand. Many of these new believers worship in music halls and some of the choice locations where Communist party members once gathered. The Word of God is being studied and shared each Sabbath in strategic locations on the main thoroughfares of that giant city.

Mark's efforts were part of a miracle of evangelistic reaping that has swept through the former Soviet Union. The gospel has spread like wildfire. It's a story that involves other evangelists and leaders from America, such as Dan Matthews of *Faith for Today*, John Carter of the *Carter Report*, and the Three Angels Broadcasting Network as well. Inspiring reports from all of these men have also thrilled hearts and encouraged the church.

The new world division that encompasses the former Soviet Union, called the Euro-Asia Division, is well organized under the leadership of Ted Wilson, son of our former General Conference president, Neal Wilson.

Mark Finley is in full control of *It Is Written* now, and his splendid presentations are combined with those of Daniel Reband, our Russian speaker, who appears on the telecast once a month.

While in Moscow, I had the privilege of seeing how God's promise in Isaiah 65:24—"before they call, I will answer"—has been fulfilled dramatically. Because, believe it or not, the Communist system is actually responsible for some of the success of this new explosion in Christian outreach. The totalitarian government used radio and television as part of their effort to control the population. Therefore, in the past, a plain but well-built radio was *given* to every family in the Soviet Union. And television sets were highly subsidized. Now these electronic instruments are *ours* to reach the hearts of those viewers. Praise God!

Peter Kulakov, the brilliant young speaker for the *Voice of Hope,* now directs this vital work in television and radio. When I first visited Russia, the media outreach was headquartered in the city of Tula, a large city about three hours' drive south of Moscow. I was moved by the dedication of our people in this humble workplace, a small one-story, three-room house with scarcely room for the manager, the treasurer, and the faithful workers who were handling the mailings in the Bible School. I actually had to bend over to get through the doorway of this tumbled-down build-ing where wallpaper had been plastered over the crumbling walls to keep them intact.

But today the Adventist Media Center in Rus-sia is housed in a new three-story building with studios and workplaces in abundance. It is a monument to the vision of many who see the vast potential for media outreach in that great land. I was present and participated when Pas-tor Robert Folkenberg, president of the denomi-nation; Ted Wilson, president of the division; and Peter Kulakov dedicated this splendid facility.

May I close this recital of Russia's historic move toward Christ with two precious testimonies— one from Mark's Moscow meetings and one from my television work in Europe.

Viktor, a tall, highly trained officer in the Russian military, made his way through a crowd of people to the back of the stage and to one of the Kremlin Congress Hall dressing rooms. Mark Finley was resting there between sessions; he was conducting two meetings a day for the people who crowded into that great assembly room. Viktor waited until he could speak to one of Mark's assistants and then told him of his urgent need to see the speaker personally.

When he was ushered into the dressing room, Viktor's hands trembled. His lips quivered. Tears flowed from his eyes as he inquired, "Pastor Finley, when is the next baptism?" He then emphatically stated, "I want to be in it."

Viktor began to tell his story. "I was a Seventh-day Adventist believer over fifty years ago here in Moscow. My father was an Adventist pastor. But under pressure from the Communist system, I left the Adventist Church. I was educated by atheistic teachers. For many years now, I've been a professor of geopolitical science. My specialty was Marxism. As I taught young Communist diplomats, soldiers, and scientists the principles of Marxism, I believed that I was aiding the world, creating a new, just society for all social classes. To me, the greatest enemy was capitalism.

"But then when the Soviet Empire crumbled, my life fell apart. Can you imagine my absolute dismay when I learned that for years I had been teaching lies! My life was in shambles. I walked the streets of Moscow wondering what to do.

"And then, quite unexpectedly, I received an invitation to your meetings. What a blessing they have been! I now have a new peace, a new joy, and a reason for living." *Thank God!*

This is just one among many stories of what God has been doing in the lives of the Russian people.

Now let me give you a little picture of some of the breakthroughs in greater Europe. The church and loyal supporters across America and our fine Adventist World Radio organization have developed radio ministry to a remarkable degree throughout these many European countries. But television—that was my burden. And I could see that one great opportunity for outreach might lie with Super Channel. This network that aired programs in the English language covered the entire continent.

Huge segments of the European population are either bilingual or trilingual; many speak English. So I traveled to London's Super Channel offices and arranged to meet the owner, a member of a family that controlled an Italian music empire. We were offered an excellent time slot, but at a very heavy expense for us—$250,000 a year. So, while I looked for the funds, Ray Dabrowski, communication director at our Northern European Division office near London; John Graz of the Euro-Africa Division from Berne, Switzerland; and It Is Written manager Royce Williams organized a myriad of details so necessary for the project's success. I would love to be able to honor the two couples who supplied the necessary funds but must protect their privacy.

Thank God, we were able to procure air time on Super Channel and begin our European broadcast. We enjoyed four years of excellent exposure. Then the National Broadcasting Company here in the United States purchased Super Channel. That meant no religious programs would be permitted on the air in Europe via Super Channel in Europe.

Fortunately, satellite releases can still reach those homes. We are exploring new strategies, with even greater potential for reaching this area of the world. God is still at the helm.

How I wish you could have read the enthusiastic letters from our viewers all over Europe. Eternity alone will be able to measure what God has done for people like Susan on that continent.

You will appreciate her letter.

I happened upon your show and felt compelled to write for your publication, *What I Like About. . . .* Maybe it can help me out of my confusion. Your show drew my interest because you discussed the path illustrating the journey of the unconverted to justification. My problem is, I remain a "lost lamb" but sense that accepting Jesus as Saviour may give me the basis for living that I so frustratingly seek. Inside I feel I *want* to live through Christ, but don't know how to make Him my guidepost.

My own religious history is none to speak of. Born Catholic, I minimally practiced the faith. Then sensing something was missing in my life, half-heartedly attended the local United Church of Christ sporadically. I guess it frustrates me to see those surrounding me secure in a faith that I am still seeking. It seemed hypocritical to pray to something that I personally have not found. Now, after two years in Switzerland, I'm 28 and still lost religiously.

I continue to feel an emptiness in terms of what is to guide my life. I've suffered no crises to mention—am healthy, well-employed, and want for nothing—except a reason and foundation for living. I sense it could be Jesus I am missing, but lack the motivation or understanding to make Him my guide.

I know this letter will likely never reach your hands. Undoubtedly, your efficient staff will send me off the requested literature, and I thank them for that, but your warmth and solid conviction flowed from the TV screen and moved me. It again reminded me of the urgency of the emptiness I've come to accept.

Susan S.

CHAPTER Six

"Do We Attend Mass *Before* or *After* We Watch *It Is Written?*"

Perhaps the most exciting story I know about as I am writing this book involves what is taking place in Brazil. The words that form the title of this chapter have been repeated throughout that country; these words come from members of Parliament, from business and professional people, and from the Hollywood of Brazil. It's something many Brazilians consider each Sunday. And it indicates the incredible level of interest these people have shown in biblical truth. Recently, a Brazilian television-rating organization evaluated our viewership there. They report that ten million people in Brazil view the *It Is Written* program *each week*. It's hard to grasp such a figure.

Five years ago, a group of Adventist business and professional people in Brazil invited Glenn

Aufderhar, the president of the Media Center, and myself to attend their yearly retreat near Rio de Janeiro. No satisfactory television program had been successfully attempted—radio, yes, a splendid radio outreach with *The Voice of Prophecy*—but not television.

As a result of our talks during that weekend, these dedicated Brazilian laypeople made an enthusiastic commitment to air *It Is Written* in their country. But notice how they proceeded. Their first decision was to cover the entire nation! Not just one or two cities! And they chose just the right man to make contact with a certain network—Dr. Milton Afonso, a leading businessman among them who owned and operated the Blue Cross organization of Brazil. There, it is called "Golden Cross."

Dr. Afonso was already in the habit of spending huge sums of money each year in television advertising for his company. His commercials aired on one of the nationwide networks. So you can imagine that executives at that network listened when he came to them with a program idea. Normally, it would cost $140,000 a month to air a program weekly at a good time. The station management suggested that *It Is Written* could have it for a generous reduction of $20,000—yes, $120,000 a month. Dr. Afonso simply said, "Not enough." They came down to $100,000—"Not enough." And $80,000—"Not enough."

Finally, the manager exclaimed, "Well, then, *what will you pay?*"

Dr. Afonso answered calmly, "$40,000."

And they accepted! But that's not all. Dr. Afonso and his lovely wife, Arlete, decided to pay the full cost for the release of *It Is Written* as their contribution, each year—nearly one-half million dollars.

Dr. Afonso also pays room and board and tuition to educate six thousand Adventist youth each year. He owns and lovingly operates forty-five orphanages.

Perhaps a little caution would be appropriate here. Please don't write this believer and ask for help on some project that some of our readers might believe in, however needful it may seem. Dr. Afonso and Dr. Santana, mentioned later, give little outside of their own country simply because of the great needs there. Dr. Afonso has been instrumental in building a huge university for our youth and took us out to see this magnificent institution by helicopter. What an inspiration!

Might I slip in a choice little story about this man's obsession with soul winning. The Adventist university I have described was located near Rio de Janeiro. But he helped many Adventist youth interested in medical training to attend the city university in São Paulo. It was a splendidly equipped medical and dental center, and Dr. Afonso was using it to help train the staff needed to operate the seventy hospitals he owns. However, he was facing a problem. Our youth had to take classes and examinations on Saturday, the Bible Sabbath. Dr. Afonso tried to make special arrangements with the university administration for Seventh-day Adventist students to take the exams on another day. But no amount of appeal seemed to make any difference. Dr. Afonso even visited the president of the institution but found him adamant.

So what did he do? *He bought the university and fired the president!*

I saw this fine medical institution in São Paulo two years ago on a trip to Brazil and was shown this São Paulo city institution. What a thrill it was to meet the able Adventist president and the tall Brazilian, Andrews University–trained man who serves as dean of deans. The dean told me in splendid English that at the moment there were 140 Adventist personnel employed at the university. He had chaplains everywhere, it seemed. In fact—can you believe this—he actually built a baptistery in the huge gymnasium. Baptisteries are installed but for one purpose—welcoming precious souls into the kingdom of Christ! Praise God!

That same commitment to earnest soul winning is shared by the majority of believers in Brazil and in other parts of South America as well.

My trips to Brazil have often caused me to wonder how quickly God's work in all the world could be completed if that same sincere devotion to winning others to Christ could be seen everywhere.

One day, one of our believers there was riding a bus and sat down next to a gentleman who happened to be a former priest. He turned and smiled at the man, gave him a friendly greeting, and asked if he had ever heard of the *It Is Written* television program.

"Yes," the gentleman responded warmly.

Encouraged, our believer ventured to ask if the man would like to study the Bible course that *It Is Written* offers. Again, the gentleman smiled in return and explained that not only had he taken the course, but had been baptized into the Adventist Church and was now sharing the truths he had learned as any Adventist pastor would do.

My Brazilian friends tell me that on another recent occasion, two bishops met. One stepped into the other's office and noticed that his colleague quickly began to shuffle some papers on his desk and move them out of sight. But this visitor had seen what they were and exclaimed, "What are you trying to hide? I saw those *It Is Written* Bible lessons on your desk. I recognized them immediately because I'm studying them as well."

Let me include just one more choice story. Our Adventist business leaders in Brazil hired the finest technicians and talent to prepare the *It Is Written* release. For a script translator, they secured the services of one of Brazil's most able translators—one who has translated popular U.S. programs such as *Kojak, L.A. Law*, etc. This man spent hours with our scripts, studying the wording and content and spirit of what was said. The Spirit of God spoke to his heart, and he responded to the message. I had the privilege of baptizing him on a return trip to Brazil.

And then there's the "dubber," the person whose voice is used on the program to give the message. He is my spokesman and does his job of "lip-syncing" so well that viewers think I'm Portuguese. Believe it or not, he is Jewish. But it would bless your heart to hear this child of Abraham use my words, now spoken by him in Portuguese, with such feeling and sincere pathos. He speaks eloquently about the cross of Christ, His death, and His resurrection and makes urgent appeals for decision in these final days of earth's history.

Well, now that Mark Finley has taken over the telecast there in Brazil, let's let *him* baptize that dear man. That would be fair, wouldn't you say?

Our Brazil visit would not be complete without mentioning another couple, Dr. Luis Santana and his lovely wife, Leony. It was he who managed the entire telecast operation. And what a splendid, efficient operation it was. This couple owns shoe stores all over Brazil and have served as our other principal supporters, giving us another half million dollars yearly and also devoting endless hours of time to make it all possible. This man has hired from his own funds fifty lay Bible workers to aid in following up on those who express interest in the telecast. The latest count indicates that fifteen thousand new believers have come into the faith directly through the telecast this past year. Praise God, is all I can say!

Mark now shares the telecasts in Brazil, with our Portuguese associate, Alejandro Bullón, a very effective evangelist who speaks on the program twice a month.

During my last trip to Brazil I made special appearances with Pastor Bullón in order to help viewers make a smooth transition from my programs, which had been airing for four years, to those of Pastor Bullón. We held meetings in a huge arena seating eighteen thousand people. I spoke for just a few moments each of the four nights. But I'll never forget those brief moments or the splendid messages Pastor Bullón gave. It was so rewarding to see God drawing so many people to Himself.

Our adventures in God's work are not without a bit of humor. Our It Is Written manager, Royce Williams, was asked to accompany me on this trip to Brazil. The good people at our home office, aware of my age and the strenuous schedule, wanted to make sure I remained in good health. So Royce came along to help me personally and to keep me from too much exhausting exposure to those dear, dear friends who wanted autographs and personal conversations, etc.

Well, the Brazilian Airline Varig upgraded my seat to first class free of charge. But my colleague Royce had to travel in coach class. I was feeling a bit uncomfortable about this and so asked the first-class flight attendant if Royce could be permitted to come up and sit in the empty seat next to me.

"Oh no," was the reply. But then she added, "Let me tell you what we will do. We will send back to his seat some of the cocktails and liquor

that he would have had, had he gone first class!"
Imagine!

The Brazil breakthrough is one of the latest chapters in the great story of the gospel spreading through the whole world via television. So allow me to share a little perspective. Let me take you back to one of the earliest breakthroughs in this area of outreach.

It happened "down under" approximately ten years ago, down in the Southern Hemisphere, down in Australia and Tasmania, only a thousand miles from the South Pole.

Some of my most rewarding experiences in evangelism came through telecasts in Australia. Let me tell you about Karry Packer, for example. He was something of a playboy in Sydney. His friends thought he never had a serious thought. But somehow this young man caught my programs on his own TV network and was attracted by the message. Karry was a dynamic business-man, owner of several newspapers and a television network that covered Australia. Karry's TV news teams gave my arrival in Australia wide coverage; his cameras seemed to follow my every move. In fact, he aired our first meeting at the Sydney Fairgrounds on his network; it, too, covered the entire nation, free of charge, of course. He also invited me for an interview on their version of the *Tonight Show*.

Have you ever been apprehensive to the point of near panic? You see, for years, both at home and overseas, I had appeared on TV for short, local interviews. But this was different; I **was** supposed to engage in charming chitchat with the host. And I didn't know whether I could pull off this kind of "conversational" program. Well, I fearfully submitted—feeling a little like a sheep led out to the slaughter.

The moment came. The host began warming up the audience. He had been instructed by "the boss" to handle me "favorably"—and, bless his heart, he tried his best. He was Jewish, though not in any sense religious. But that particular night, a former host had returned for a one-night visit to his old program, and he was invited to join in the conversation. I was to confront them both. Before I came out as one of the guests, Rita Hayworth was interviewed, and she talked for a few moments about her life in the movies. (Incidentally, her father became an Adventist after viewing *It Is Written* in Florida.)

Next on the show was a segment featuring a demonstration game of fast-moving Australian soccer. Finally, I was brought on the set. I sat down in a swivel chair between the two hosts and was greeted cordially.

But then the questions began tumbling out. And they were hard-edged. The visiting host blurted out, "What do you think of Billy Graham?—I don't like him." I replied with a few favorable remarks about Billy Graham's ministry. But this man kept shooting questions—"Do you believe God sent a flood to destroy the world He says He made?"

At that point, the Jewish host, though not religious in the least, as I said, turned in fury to his visiting friend and began to defend the Old Testament, which was supposed to be his heritage. The two went at each other with animated vigor, to say the least.

In the meantime, the television station switchboard had lighted up like a Christmas tree. People from all over Australia were calling in. And almost all of them were loudly objecting to the way these two hosts were handling a very important topic.

Back on the set I breathed a prayer, took courage, and managed to interrupt the arguing hosts. "Wait a minute," I said with a smile. "You fellows are supposed to be interviewing me. All I ask is time to say just a sentence or two about this question of origins."

Of course, they sheepishly agreed. So, praying for the right words, I said, "If our ideas about origins are confused and distorted—if our ideas about the beginnings of our world are fuzzy and unclear—our conclusions about the end of all things and our future will be confused, distorted, fuzzy, and unclear as well."

Evidently the dear Lord knew that these few words in that stormy, stress-filled moment would do more good than anything else for that listening nation at that moment. We saw the results later in the deepening interest of the Australian people in the gospel.

Our telecasts in Australia were an important breakthrough. But that success raised a very important question—In these nations of the United States, Canada, and Australia, etc., where powerful networks and other stations saturate the airwaves, how do we reap the results? How do we help the hundreds of Australian pastors and the thousands of pastors in United States and Canada to turn a TV audience into personal contacts?

That question haunted George Knowles, my associate speaker, and his wife, Lillian, and Nellie and myself as we were traveling together in the States in the seventies. That's when the idea of doing seminars began to dawn. Why couldn't we do seminars on biblical topics? We could draw interested people together to spend a full day of inspiration and instruction, serve a luscious vegetarian sample dinner for them at noon, and give opportunity for the visitors to interact with a local pastor there at the seminar. This plan might well produce the most long-lasting results.

I had also been experimenting with ideas on Bible marking with an audience as a way to get those with little knowledge of the Scriptures into vital doctrinal topics. And I wanted to combine this technique with the basic seminar idea (which was actually originated by John Coltheart of Australia).

Well, the seminar concept has proven its worth. These all-day seminars spread all over the United States, Australia, and around the world. In our initial seminar ventures in the cities of Australia—Sydney, Melbourne, Brisbane, Adelaide, and Perth—we found that the people and the pastors responded beautifully. We carried the strategy to cities throughout the United States. We found that our seminars in the major cities were drawing, at times, in excess of two thousand eager participants. In one season alone, Jim and Erma Todd sent twenty-two tons of Bibles, lessons, and other items across America. They also traveled to Australia and expertly organized other seminar programs there.

Let me tell you about Los Angeles. We were concerned that this metropolis posed special challenges. The movie capital of the world has so much that attracts the attention of the people. We knew that we would have to do something unusual.

So we chose to hold our seminar on the *Queen Mary*, dry-docked permanently at the harbor in Long Beach. Seven hundred and fifty people came to the sessions on Saturday and Sunday.

But these first ventures in conducting religious seminars were not without their "birth pangs." We planned to give our participants copies of the Bible, which Sam Martz, a publisher in Nashville, would provide. The Bibles were ordered in plenty of time but somehow got lost between trucking lines in the Southeast. The Friday night before the first Saturday seminar session, Nellie and I had boarded the *Queen Mary* and were occupying a stateroom. We worked the phone furiously all evening to trace the "lost" Bibles. We finally tracked them down to the Continental Can Company. They were still on their truck in Tennessee early Friday evening. But, believe it or not, on Sabbath morning, they arrived at the Los Angeles Airport. Connie and her boy-

friend were at the airport the moment they arrived, and our staff was tearing open the boxes
just as the people walked into the ship for the
seminar. Opening day was saved with not a moment to spare. The situation had been very tense,
but we were so happy about how it all worked
out that my associate, George Knowles, and I
set to work just as if we were both twenty years
younger and could handle the strain.

One other memorable incident that happened
at that seminar relates to my family. Ron, our
son who has been ill, you may remember, was
living at home at the time and wanted to attend
the seminar. Once on the ship, he disappeared
for part of the day without anyone noticing that
he was gone. When he returned, Ron told me
that he had been searching the ship for the secret passageway that he and his brother George
had found when we first sailed on the *Queen
Mary* to London many years earlier. Ron con-
fessed that this passageway took the boys to the
first-class section—forbidden territory to coach
passengers. So this was where they'd been when
"off playing"! Sometimes it's better when you
don't find out about your children's little mis-
chief until a few years have passed.

The seminar outreach just kept growing and
developing. We conducted a teleseminar in 1981.
Our live seminar presentations in Los Angeles
were sent via satellite hookup to twenty large
American and Canadian cities, where six thousand people participated. Los Angeles Mayor Tom
Bradley opened the event at the Beverly Hilton

Hotel. I conducted the full-day seminar along with Lonnie Melashenko, my associate at the time. Paul Harvey joined us from Phoenix, Arizona, for a panel discussion on health. Only President Reagan and our Mormon friends had tried this teleseminar idea before. It seemed like a bold venture at the time, and there were many worries, but God blessed the results.

Now in 1995, Mark Finley has led out in a far more advanced version of the same plan—NET '95. This full five-week series of evangelistic meetings originated in Chattanooga, Tennessee. Some eight hundred churches hosted these same presentations via satellite. Some ten thousand made commitments to Christ in baptism as a result. Mark hopes to see this plan embracing several continents at one time in the near future. Again, let me say with all my heart, Praise God from whom *all* blessings flow.

CHAPTER
Seven

Who Tore Up the Telephone Book?

Few countries have yielded so rich and exciting a story as has Israel. Some of the most unforgettable events in my ministry took place in that land. Among them:

- The on-camera discovery of a Dead Sea artifact.

- Coming into possession of a portion of one of the Dead Sea Scrolls.

- Witnessing firsthand the first Constitutional Congress that declared Israel a state.

- Encounters with Yigael Yadin, the deputy prime minister of Israel and

world-renowned archaeologist; in fact,
the restorer of Masada.

The story begins a few decades ago on my first
filming expedition to Jordan. We were hoping to
get interesting footage of archaeological excavations at the Qumran Caves along the shore of
the Dead Sea. Two men accompanied us there:
King Hussein's director of antiquities and Father Roland de Vaux, a Dominican priest and
archaeologist who was assisting the Jordanians
in evaluating and preserving the valuable artifacts discovered at the Qumran Caves.

This particular site had drawn world attention some years ago because of the providential discovery of the Dead Sea Scrolls there.
Two Bedouin boys had been tending some
sheep amid the dry hills near the Dead Sea.
One of them idly threw a stone into an opening on the side of a steep hill. The boys heard
the sound of cracking pottery inside the cave.
This terrified them, and they fled for their lives.
However, some time later, their curiosity over-
came their fear. The boys returned to the site,
climbed the hill, and discovered the original
Dead Sea Scrolls packed tightly in clay jars.
They took one of these jars, which happened
to have the Isaiah Scroll inside, and somehow
brought it down the rough terrain to their village. There, they rolled the scroll out carefully
to its full twenty-eight-foot length. Eventually,
they took this leather roll to Kando, a shoe-
maker in Bethlehem. Thinking it would be help-

ful in his shoe business, he purchased it for a pittance.

Fortunately, rumors of this discovery reached the ears of Professor Sukenik. This archaeologist was something of a hero in Israel. He had endangered his life in the Israeli/Arab war, crawling under a barbed-wire fence and through enemy fire on an important mission during the heat of battle. Professor Sukenik decided to check out this discovery. He made the trip safely to Bethlehem and discovered to his astonishment that this roll of leather contained almost the entire Hebrew text of the book of Isaiah.

This single discovery has taken scholarship nearly a thousand years nearer the original manuscript of the Old Testament. In other words, it was a thousand years older than any copy of the Bible then in existence.

This is why I was so eager to take a film crew to the site of the Qumran Caves, still being excavated. I was quite young and full of enthusiasm. I found myself leaping across a chasm to the opening of Cave Number 4, where the scrolls had been found. (After I made the leap, I also wondered how I could ever return safely from that perilous height.)

But in that visit to Cave Number 4 I looked down and saw something that led to the title of this chapter: Who Tore Up the Telephone Book? That question comes from a story about a scholar from the state of Virginia who took his little boy on an expedition to examine Cave

Number 4. The lad was especially struck by what covered the cave floor—hundreds of broken pieces of scroll that had been carelessly trampled on in the process of taking more valuable ones to Bethlehem. The young lad looked at the mass of torn scroll fragments, several inches deep, and exclaimed, "Who tore up the telephone book?"

Well, we realized that what had been preserved for millennia in this cave was something more eternal than a phone book. It was, in fact, God's message to us through Scripture. We followed those scroll fragments to what is now called the Rockefeller Museum, where scholars painstakingly assembled hundreds of bits of parchment, reconstructing portions of the original scrolls like a giant jigsaw puzzle.

But we were also able to return to the Qumran site with our cameras and record a new discovery at this historic site. Roland de Vaux had just opened another "dig" in the ruins of the Qumran community and was uncovering valuable artifacts. He urged us to join him with our cameras.

No bulldozers or even picks or shovels were used at the site, of course. He was carefully uncovering pottery shards and other artifacts with his fingers, gently removing dirt with a simple camel-hair brush. We taped a microphone under Father de Vaux's long beard and rolled the cameras as he described what he was doing. His eyes sparkled with delight at the thought of our recording his historic find at this new "dig."

I actually had my first glimpse of Israel some

years before this filming expedition. I was headed to India, on my first overseas trip, to train our pastors there and found I could purchase a ticket that took me around the world at no extra cost. I made sure that one of my stops would be in Palestine.

The war between the Israelis and Arabs was still going on at the time. I had to cross from Jordan into Israel through a "no man's land" bordered by barbed wire. Porters accompanied me from the U.S. Embassy, carrying my luggage. But as soon as they got to the edge of the barbed entanglement, they dropped everything and fled back to safety. I picked up the bags and managed to make my way carefully across the wilderness of barbed wire, emerging on the Israeli side just a few feet from the famed King David Hotel. (It was here that many a historic treaty was signed as flare-up after flare-up continued through those stormy years.)

At that time, my travel per diem was set at $3 per day. So I decided to "blow it" on just one meal at this famed hotel. After very slowly enjoying a nice dinner, I stood at the entrance savoring the experience of actually being in Jerusalem, that holy city with its incredible history.

Suddenly, a limousine filled with important-looking New York Jewish gentlemen drove up to the entrance and took on a passenger or two. The men turned to me standing there and invited me to join them. This was in May 1948, and they were headed to the convention that was about to declare Israel a sovereign state.

Well, you may be sure, I accepted their invitation gladly. These gracious leaders took me with them into the VIP section of the convention. There, I was given earphones so I could hear all the proceedings of that historic event in my own language.

Years later, I had the opportunity to interview the deputy prime minister of Israel, Yigael Yadin, at the Jerusalem Hilton Hotel for one of our *It Is Written* programs. We wanted to ask him about his work as an archaeologist in restoring Masada. (Mr. Yadin was the son of Dr. Sukenik, who discovered the book of Isaiah in that leather scroll from the Qumran caves.)

Mr. Yadin and I had a delightful conversation. He was very interested in my experience at the convention hall on that historic occasion when Israel became a state. I also talked of my visits to excavations at the Qumran Caves and at Masada. Afterward, he declared, "I remember all of these occasions and to think you lived through them just as I did."

Well, that day cemented a relationship with him that finally climaxed in my giving him a piece of the Dead Sea Scrolls that had providentially come into my hands. Even small portions of the scrolls were immensely valuable. The one that had come into my possession had been examined and confirmed authentic by Dr. William Foxwell Albright, the eminent archaeologist of Johns Hopkins University. After all the wonderful things I had experienced in Israel and been able to share with *It Is Written* viewers, it seemed a small act of thanks to give this fragment back to the state of Israel.

Dr. Siegfried Horn, an archaeologist from Andrews University, was a long-time friend and associate of Yigael Yadin. They had participated in several Israeli "digs" through the years. Dr. Horn also felt that we had done the wise thing by placing this choice piece of Israeli history, and sacred history, in the hands of that country's preeminent archaeologist.

Dr. Yadin's exploits in restoring the site of ancient Masada could fill several volumes. It was at Masada that the last Hebrew patriots fighting against Roman oppression after the fall of Jerusalem in A.D. 70 lost their lives. They had occupied this mountaintop fortress that Herod the Great had built near the shores of the Dead Sea. The defenders of Masada held out for some time against assaults by Roman soldiers. Finally, the Romans, you may remember, built a ramp and battering ram to attack the fortress. But when they finally succeeded in breaking through, they found all of the defenders dead by their own hands—except a couple of women who had hidden and survived to tell the story.

Through the years, many of my choicest memories have come from the occasional Holy Land tours we led to these sacred places. Nellie has been able to share them too. We always found a warm welcome in Israel. Certain Jewish authorities had hoped that as a television evangelist I would use my influence to bring some degree of understanding between the "hardliners" of Jewish sectarianism and those who wanted to bridge the exclusiveness and bring more understanding between Jews and Christians.

It was this concern that led these friends among Israeli authorities one day to persuade the rabbi at the Western Wall to place his blessing on our tour group. That was a treasured experience and a gracious breakthrough. Hopefully, more such meetings can be enjoyed.

In all our Israeli experiences, one underlying vision prevailed. It was here that on a certain "black Friday" about two thousand years ago our Saviour stood trial in the Sanhedrin chamber. There, Nicodemus defended him, and Gamaliel urged caution with his now-famous words: "If this counsel or this work be of men, it will come to nought: but if it be of God, ye cannot overthrow it; lest haply ye be found even to fight against God" (Acts 5:38, 39).

That's good counsel for us even today.

Another unforgettable experience took place in the street of Old Jerusalem known as the Way of the Cross. We had arrived at the Ecce Homo Arch (*ecce homo* refers to Pilate's words "Behold the Man"). Hundreds of years ago, a Christian penitent built a convent on the site where the soldiers played their games of dice as Jesus was condemned. You can still see one of their games carved in the stone.

We were blessed with a very cordial friendship with the mother superior there, the one in complete charge of this oft-visited location. We ventured to ask if we could film this historic spot for our television program. She graciously consented.

Well, as we tried to light the rather dim indoor scene for our cameras, we blew fuse after fuse of the convent's rather primitive electrical system. But the long-suffering mother superior continued to cooperate until we succeeded. There was more evidence of Christ in that place than just ancient stones.

Probably the most familiar of the sacred places for those who have visited Palestine is the Garden Tomb. We cannot with certainty point to this picturesque garden and tomb as the actual place where Christ was placed after His death. But all scholars agree that this ancient tomb is certainly very much like one in which Christ would have been laid. And it is for that reason so many visit, explore, and worship there, conducting quiet Communion services to seal the blessed experience in the Holy Land and their own personal commitment to Christ. Usually, there are from four to eight groups in the Garden Tomb area at any given time, holding their special services and then filing quietly past the opening to the tomb.

However, our groups were so large that we had to plan ahead and reserve the entire garden. We conducted Communion services for one hundred pilgrims, sometimes as many as two hundred. Then, just after we'd raised the cup representing Christ's sacrificial blood to our lips, Dan and Marilyn Cotton, standing by the tomb in the distance, would sing in their beautiful voices "Up From the Grave He Arose." Then in the afterglow of that experience, the entire group would pass by or enter the tomb one by one as our staff would help them.

I thank God that discoveries which illuminate events in the Bible continue to be made in that exciting land. For instance, in the Jewish Quarter of Jerusalem, you can now see among the excavations the remains of the Cardo, a street from Roman times. You can also view a portion of a wall dating to the first temple era and the ruins of a house that was burned around A.D. 70. That house was the home of a priest named Katros. And, believe it or not, archaeologists have concluded that this man was misusing his sacred office. Certain artifacts found on the site suggest that he was producing and/or using counterfeit materials in the sacrificial services. "Be sure your sin will find you out"—even if it doesn't happen until thousands of years later!

We entered one beautiful five-thousand-square-foot house. I came to the conclusion that this edifice, with its mosaic floors that looked like magnificent carpeting, was a house very much like the house that Nicodemus would have owned and used as his base of operations in helping the infant church. Whether it was his house or not, we do know that he must have owned something like it because of his immense assistance to the early church. Who does not remember Nicodemus's historic meeting with Jesus that took place at night, when he was confronted with those soul-searching words: "Verily, verily, I say unto thee, Except a man be born again, he cannot see the kingdom of God" (John 3:3).

Eight

Solving
the Riddle

I t just could be that you are one of my many
friends who have heard of my interest in
solving the riddle of Ararat. And you may be
wondering *why*. Well, simply put—it was my driving ambition to attract the attention of an unbe-
lieving world and to turn their minds back to
the God of the Bible and the basic truths surrounding the creation of our world and the flood
of Noah's day.

Several times, these two truths are connected,
in fact, vitally connected, in Scripture. The
apostle Peter even ties in these two truths with
the second coming of Jesus:

> Knowing this first, that there shall come
> in the last days scoffers, walking after their
> own lusts, and saying, Where is the

promise of his coming? for since the fathers fell asleep, all things continue as they were from the beginning of the creation. For this they willingly are ignorant of, that by the word of God the heavens were of old, and the earth standing out of the water and in the water: whereby the world that then was, being overflowed with water, perished: but the heavens and the earth, which are now, by the same word are kept in store, reserved unto fire against the day of judgment and perdition of ungodly men (2 Peter 3:3-7).

However wild and controversial such a concept as my interest in Ararat might seem to my conservative friends, one must at least credit me with sincerity. You see, unfortunately, a growing number of adventurers in climbing Ararat—well-meaning though they may have been—have been the object of ridicule. I realized that my interest could be so judged as well. Would it be worth the risk?

I knew that to minimize that risk I would need to confine my participation to working with valid professional partners, following up substantial leads. And one of those "leads" came to me on December 29, 1959. I was on the faculty of Emmanuel Missionary College at the time. "Sit down," I said to a colleague. "Listen to this!"

This is a translation from the German—*Staats Zeitung und Herald*—(well, you pronounce it)—Woodside, New Jersey, on November 15. It is titled "Stereo Air Photos at Mt. Ararat Show Petrified Boat

Possibly Noah's Ark of the Bible." It's a Columbus, Ohio, release, and here is what it says:

If Noah's Ark is really at Mt. Ararat in Turkey, then there is a discovery from a young Turk who is living in Columbus, Ohio. Serket Kurtis has stereographic air photos that he made in Turkey from which maps can be produced.

The "discovery" has not yet been verified. However, Kurtis assumes that the curious form of the discovered object could be the ark of Noah, which is described in the Bible and in the Koran. (Kurtis is a faithful Mohammedan.)

The air photos were taken a year ago on behalf of the Geodetic Institute of Turkey. It was discovered when in Ankara by Captain Ilhan Durupinar who used a stereoplanograph beneath the wings of his plane in order to prepare maps. With this instrument this object was discovered, which could not have been created by nature itself but by human hands.

Dr. Arthur Brandenberger of the Geodetic Institute of Ohio State University said after he had seen the stereophotos he also is convinced that this discovery cannot be a "product of nature," but possibly a "petrified boat."

I put the paper down and waited for comment. Little did I know what would come of this. But I had begun to realize, even then, that I was handling a piece of an agelong jigsaw puzzle that might or might not fit.

"Is there any way of checking the story?"

"Difficult," I said. "Turkey."

"But look. This Dr. Brandenberger that it mentions here is at Ohio State University."

I thought fast. And perhaps I was impulsive when I lifted the phone. But in a few minutes I was talking with Dr. Brandenberger. I found him approachable, friendly, and a little more than curiously interested.

Here was a man ranking high in his field—a photogrammetry expert. Yet according to the article, he had already committed himself to the suggestion that a huge boat might be preserved near Ararat.

Now to save you the suspense, I'll tell you quickly. After weeks of planning, decision making, arrangements, and travel, Dr. Siegfried Horn, an archaeologist I had known and trusted, agreed to travel to Turkey and participate in the verification in company with Dr. Arthur Brandenberger himself and Captain Durupinar, the aerial photographer. Don Loveridge from Florida financed the trip. We were finally on our way with several other intensely interested individuals.

We stopped in London and secured the favorable interest of the British Museum's director of Middle East antiquities. We spent considerable time in Ankara awaiting permission and the cooperation of Turkey's director of antiquities. The army officers were ready when we arrived at Dogubayazit. They were led on horseback by Captain Baykel. Now, what did we discover? What was the result of all this activity?

It was soon discovered that the site did not prove to be of significant value. The scientists carefully dug out a spot along the edge, but this test yielded nothing of particular interest. Much to the chagrin of Dr. Horn, the soldiers dynamited the spot that had been so carefully dug—no archaeologist would do such a thing!

The *Encyclopaedia Britannica* Yearbook of 1960 carried this story with pictures of the "boat."

By now, however, information, historical narratives, facts, and rumor tumbled into our thinking like an avalanche.

I discovered in my study during the next few years that we were not the only ones who through the centuries had attempted to solve the riddle. Some had sought it through carefully planned expeditions. Others had found evidence through sheer providence—which leads me to tell you about Haji—his story is evidence of pure providence.

I kept thinking of Haji. There he lay—alone, seriously ill, in the upper room of an abandoned mansion in Oakland, California. The year was 1915.

A tiny window was open beside his cot. Through it, he could hear the familiar start and stop of traffic along Telegraph Avenue. Help was so near. But even if he could raise himself to the window, his weak voice could never be heard above the din.

There was no telephone. Once, when he first became ill, he had tried to make it down the stairs to find help and food. But he had had to turn back to his cot.

No one would ever find him now. The grass had grown high on the once beautifully land-scaped grounds. No passing salesman now would be attracted to the big house set back from the street. But then, if he died, it wouldn't matter to anyone. Besides, he was so tired. So tired!

Haji Yearam had lived an eventful life. As a boy he had lived at the foot of Mount Ararat. Then as a young man he had made a pilgrimage on foot from Ararat to Jerusalem, earning the title of *haji*, or "pilgrim." The name *Yearam* is Armenian for "Jeremiah." Jeremiah the pilgrim. Later in life he had become a merchant in the city of Constantinople.

It is of interest to note that he became a Christian after meeting J. N. Andrews, one of the first Seventh-day Adventist missionaries in Europe.

But now, at the age of seventy-four and grow-ing blind, he lay desperately ill in this abandoned mansion. The rooms of the big house were used to store pieces of antique furniture that he had hoped to sell one day.

Silently, weakly, he prayed for help. And then, his strength gone, he lapsed into unconscious-ness. For hours the little room was still.

Would he die without telling his strange story? Was it to be forever sealed, forever lost with the memory of a man who for more than threescore and ten years had kept his secret under threat of death?

Evidently it was to be otherwise.

A little way down Telegraph Avenue, Harold Williams had stopped by to visit his parents. He was attending a college seventy miles north at Angwin, California. And he and his wife were operating a small nursing home near the school to pay expenses. Today, he had brought a patient into the city and planned to spend a little time with his parents.

He had been in the house only a short time when a boy arrived with a message from the family pastor, who had learned of his presence. Would Harold be so kind as to drop by a certain address and see if he could locate a man by the name of Haji Yearam? He had been absent from church for several weeks, and it was feared he might be ill. And if such should be the case, Harold, with his medical background, perhaps could help him.

The address was easily located, but he could find no sign of life in the building or on the grounds of this overgrown estate. His loud rapping brought no response. Could this be the right address? He was about to leave. But no. A sick man might not be able to answer.

Finding the door unlocked, he went through all the rooms and up flights of stairs until finally he did find Haji on his cot by the window—alone, unconscious, almost dead.

He was too ill to be moved. It was necessary to remain with him for a time. Then he took him to his parents' home and later to his own home near the college, where he and his wife cared for him as he recovered, though he grew more and more blind until he lost his sight completely.

Haji was deeply appreciative of all that was done for him. He tried to show his gratitude by deeding to Mrs. Williams a house that he owned. But they felt it a privilege to have the dear elderly man in their home. "Haji," said Harold Williams, "was one of the most dedicated men I ever knew."

Then one day Haji made a strange request. "Harold, he said, "if you're going to the store, I wish you would bring back a new composition book. And be sure you have a good pencil or pen."

There were no idle words with Haji. When he spoke, you knew he had something important to say. The composition book was purchased, and Haji asked Mrs. Williams, also, to come in. What could be on his mind?

"Now take some scratch paper first," he said. "I have something that I must tell you before I die. I want you to write down exactly what I say, for I believe that someday this information will be very important."

Harold wrote it all down and read it back. Haji corrected it. Three times it was written down and corrected as it was read. Haji wanted to be sure every word was right. Then it was carefully copied in the composition book and read back again, and Haji signed it. Harold and his wife signed as witnesses and were made to promise that when the proper time should come, the information would be given to those who would use it wisely.

And this was Haji's story:

Haji had lived at the foot of greater Mount Ararat, as I said. His parents, according to Armenian tradition, were directly descended from those who had come out of the ark and who had never migrated over into the land of Shinar with others who built the Tower of Babel or with still others who had migrated to various countries. Haji's forefathers had always remained near the mount, where not far down from the summit the ark had come to rest in a little valley surrounded by small mountain peaks.

For hundreds of years after the Flood, his forefathers had made yearly pilgrimages up the mountain to the ark to worship. This practice stopped abruptly centuries ago when a terrific storm interrupted their journeys. They believed this was a sign of God's displeasure.

Sometimes in an especially hot summer, a shepherd or a wandering hunter would report seeing the prow of the ark protruding from the ice. They knew that it was there. And they believed that someday, when the time was right, a divine hand would reveal its presence to the world.

It was when Haji was about fourteen years of age that he shared in the amazing experience he had never dared to tell.

Haji's father had on occasion served as a guide. One day, three strangers came to his home and hired him to take them up the slopes of Ararat.

They hired the boy to assist him.

It was not until they were on their way that they made known the purpose of their expedition. These three men, it seems, were scientists from London, England, and were bitter atheists. They did not believe the Bible account of the Flood of Noah's day and were determined once for all to prove it untrue. They had heard reports that the ark still existed. Now they wished to comb the mountain carefully and then use the unfruitfulness of their search as an argument to convince the world that the ark did not exist and that the Flood never happened.

Haji's father was naturally taken aback at this. He remembered the traditions that had come down through his family. What should he do? Should he guide these strangers on such a mission?

The impulse was strong within him to show these self-confident men that they were wrong. He knew the ark was there. He knew right where to take them. Should he do it? Perhaps, he reasoned—perhaps it was now the time that Providence wished to make known the presence of the ark.

So Haji and his father led the way. After considerable hardship and peril, they reached a little valley not far down from the summit, a valley surrounded by smaller mountain peaks. And there it was! There, protruding from the ice, was the prow of a mighty ship! At one side of the valley, the waters from the melting ice spilled over into a little river that ran down the mountain.

It was an exceptionally hot summer, and the

ice had melted back far enough to expose the great door in the side of the ship, or rather the opening where the door had been. The door itself had been taken off and hauled a little distance up the mountain, where it formed the roof for an altar of worship.

Haji and his father watched the faces of these confused men. They entered the ark and explored it carefully. They found rooms of various sizes, some of them with great strong bars, as if for animals of different kinds. They took measurements. Everything checked with the Genesis description of the ark. The entire structure was covered, outside and inside, with a sort of varnish or lacquer that was very thick and strong. It was built like a mighty house on the hull of a ship, but without any windows.

The scientists were appalled and dumbfounded. They were uncontrollably angry at finding what they had hoped to prove nonexistent. They had only hand axes, guns, and knives, and with these they tried furiously to destroy the boat. But what could they do with hand axes against a mighty ship? It was like chopping at a thunderstorm.

Then they tried to burn it. But it would not burn. The wood was not like our wood today, but more like stone.

They were completely defeated. In their fury, the three of them vowed that not one of them would ever reveal what they had found. Then they turned to the boy and his father. "We'll keep check on you too."

Haji had been about fourteen then. Now he was seventy-five. He and his father had never told the experience except to the most trusted relatives. But now his father was dead. The scientists, being much older than Haji, must be dead by now. Certainly at this date, there could be no danger in revealing the truth. And he had a deep conviction that the time would come when this information would be useful.

Harold Williams tells me that he asked Haji if he still knew the way to the ark, if he could take him to the spot.

"Yes," he said. "If I had my eyes."

That is the story. Was the old man's memory playing tricks? Was he the victim of hallucinations? How, then, can we account for the uncanny similarity between Haji's story and that of the Russians who sighted the boat in 1916 and visited it in 1917? Both specifically mention that the door of the ark was missing and describe an altar of worship built from the missing timbers. Yet when Haji told his story, the Russian experience was still future. And careful checking reveals that the author of the Russian story knew nothing whatever of Haji.

Could such a fantastic tale as Haji's be true?

Listen to this. In May 1916, Harold Williams and his wife moved to South Lancaster, Massachusetts. And in September of 1917 they moved to the little city of Brockton, not far from Boston. One morning at breakfast, he tells me, he sat reading the paper. And there at the bottom of the front page was a news item one column wide and perhaps several inches deep. Its headline attracted his attention, for it made some mention of the ark.

The story told of an aged scientist on his deathbed in the city of London. He had told those about him that he was afraid to die without making an urgent confession. He then related to them how he had come upon the ark in company with two other scientists, who were now dead. He told of their vow of secrecy.

Haji, totally blind, had been left with Harold Williams's parents in Oakland and was now dead. But Harold and his wife still had the notebook in which they had recorded his story. Eagerly, they took it out and compared his account with that of the scientist on his deathbed. The dates, the places, the people were the same. The two accounts checked in every detail. They had never doubted Haji's story. But here was unexpected and complete corroboration of it.

I could not forget Haji's story. It made too much sense. And I kept asking myself, "If the ark was still there in 1854, and if it was still there in 1883—and in 1916—and possibly in 1952—could it not be there today—at least some trace of it?

It would not be wise, considering the scope of this book, to detail the considerable activity that has been ongoing to this date—with which I have had nothing to do.

So, this is "my" story of the riddle—only the dear Lord knows how and when He will unfold it more fully. I'll be patient for "the rest of the story."

CHAPTER
Nine

The President
Needs You!

S urely you and I have been inspired by the apostle Paul's enthusiastic reference to converts from his ministry among the members of Caesar's household (see Philippians 4:22). It is evident his heart was gladdened that the message of the cross had found its way into the imperial palace, not because it gave him reason for selfish pride, but because of the advantage for the spread of the gospel through this channel at the seat of the Roman Empire.

Somewhat the same choice sense of satisfaction has been mine as opening after opening has afforded a privileged opportunity to witness at the home of the United States Presidents—the White House—and to develop friendships within its walls.

Presidents Gerald Ford, Ronald Reagan, and

George Bush each extended invitations for me to come to the White House for briefings. I met with them either in the Roosevelt Room or the Cabinet chambers and on occasion had personal contacts in the Oval Office.

The pertinent questions asked—the counsel sought by these men and their aides—were sincere and penetrating. It warmed my heart to know that these men felt they needed our input.

Let me tell you how these occasions became more personal and helpful. It happened on the day we all gathered for the inauguration of President George Bush. Nellie and I were invited to the inaugural ceremonies.

On the inaugural day, Nellie and I and other invitees assembled at a hotel location a number of miles from the Capitol and boarded a designated White House bus that carried us through the crowds to the Capitol. The women were then separated from the men and taken to a vantage point in front of the inaugural platform. We men were taken to the actual roof of the Capitol, the left roof facing the central speaker's stand.

On the roof, the state governors were seated in the first four rows. Then came three rows of religious leaders, and behind us the extended Bush family. We were told that eleven highchairs had to be brought into the White House dining room that morning for breakfast. The older children were, of course, seated next to the President and Mrs. Bush. But the rest were just behind us.

We were seated up to the edge of the roof. A

scaffolding had been erected between the left wing and the right wing of the Capitol to hold hundreds of seats. From that point down to the President, the senators and their families and the House legislators and their families were seated.

Dr. Lloyd Ogilvie of the Fifth Avenue Presbyterian Church, a popular television personality, sat by me on my left, Pastor Neal Wilson on my right. May I say at this point that Lloyd Ogilvie is a man whom I deeply admire—sincere, genuine, and able, a great Scottish preacher with a nationwide audience. He is highly respected among his peers. Since that time, this fine man has been chosen as the chaplain of the United States Senate.

But that morning, Dr. Ogilvie was shivering with a threat of a fever. He turned to me and asked if I would take his next Sunday television service if he came down with a serious sickness. He was well enough to continue, but the thought of his confidence and friendship was a choice memory.

Following the ceremony, the men and women were all united for a White House luncheon in the War Memorial Building and then placed on the first four rows of the parade route next to the presidential enclosure. The warm association with those other religious leaders on that cold day is also a special memory. Jesse Jackson and, especially, his wife were the source of much hilarious humor. Dr. James Kennedy and Dr. James Dobson, their wives, and Nellie and I took ample advantage of the occasion during the intervals of the parade to deepen our friendship.

It was on that cold January twentieth that I met Douglas Wead, the President's religious advisor, and a long and fruitful relationship began.

More recently, we asked Doug Wead to speak at each of several yearly partnership gatherings—Washington, D.C., Orlando, Florida, and Los Angeles. On one of these occasions, he said:

> I knew that George Bush would love George Vandeman because they are very much alike in many ways. They are both very understated, very cool. I think George Vandeman might have an edge over the President as a television personality, but he's had a little more practice there. But both are absolute gentlemen, and they have gotten along just great. And, Dr. Vandeman, we appreciate the input, advice, and counsel you've given this White House. They're lucky to have you there at the President's side to offer that help and insight. The President needs you.
>
> I remember we had these little prayer get-togethers, a few of us, our senior staff early in the morning on Fridays. And I remember one Friday we were having our prayer devotion together, and we were pretty concerned about some of the trends and the drifts that have been taking place in this country, particularly

the size of government. We talked of our worship, when and how you want to worship, without government stepping in and becoming theologians and deciding it's going to be Sunday instead of Saturday. Especially you Adventists, you know something of this very real threat to religious liberty in this country. They were concerned, just as you would have been.

One day at our White House prayer group, we passed Pastor Vandeman's book around—the one about *What I Like About . . . .* And what was interesting to me was that the Baptists would read two chapters—the chapter about the Baptists—to see what he was going to say, how fair he would be, how wrong he would be, how right he would be—and the chapter on Adventists. And the same was true of the Lutherans, the Charismatics, and everybody else. And because of the spirit of love and appreciation and kindness, the spirit of Christ, in Dr. Vandeman's personality and his speaking and his writing, people are interested in just what he believes and what you Adventists have to offer the body of Christ. It was exciting to see this wholesome and animated reaction.

One person always welcome at the President's side was Billy Graham. For that reason, I have chosen to include him in this "presidential chapter." I'm not sure about the date of my first meeting with Billy Graham. Nellie and I actually attended his huge crusade at the Herringay Arena in London—his first giant meeting of this kind—but didn't meet him personally then.

It was in later years that I was invited to be with him on the stage at the new Madison Square Garden Stadium. And when we met in the prayer session, before we entered the stage area, he hugged me so tightly with his big frame that I could scarcely breathe. He was so very warm in his evaluation of the It Is Written ministry. In fact, on one occasion he quoted from my book *Planet in Rebellion* seventeen times for one of his messages. He gave me credit, of course, but that indicated he'd been doing some extensive reading.

Really, there were two people who were instrumental in drawing Billy Graham and me closer together. One was Paul Harvey. The other was Emilio Knechtle. Billy Graham's wife, Ann, was a classmate of Mrs. Knechtle and a close friend of many, many years.

Paul Harvey told me thirty-three years ago that Billy Graham had two stacks of *The Desire of Ages* four feet high—all given to him by well-meaning Seventh-day Adventists who thought he had none. How many do you suppose he has today after another thirty-three years? I wonder! At least we know that this dear man had ample opportunity to examine this precious, unexcelled book on the life of Jesus.

And my last "hug" with him was at the fortieth anniversary of the Los Angeles six-pole tent meeting when William Randolph Hearst told his reporters to "puff Graham up," a slang expression for exposing him to world recognition. And, of course, it worked.

It is very interesting how God works and whom He uses in the grand work of salvation during these closing moments of our world's history.

I prayerfully hope that my contacts with these unusual men from "Caesar's household," in particular, will prove eternally helpful.

Ten

Memorable
Moments

In this final chapter, I'd like to look back on some of the most unusual and delightful moments in my years of ministry. I'm so grateful for the special people God has brought into my life and for the memorable and providential events that resulted in transformed lives.

I've always been fascinated by stories involving how some of our favorite Christian hymns came to be written. So it came as a surprise to find myself personally involved in the continuing saga surrounding one particular hymn, "It Is Well With My Soul," written by Chicago attorney Horatio Spafford. Here's how it happened.

It all began some time ago with Dwight L. Moody, the Spirit-endowed, down-to-earth evangelist, whose huge Chicago tabernacle was destroyed in a citywide fire. Horatio Spafford and his wife were especially liberal supporters of Moody's ministry. Unfortunately, their home burned to the ground in the Chicago fire as well. Horatio immediately sent his wife and their four children to France, where they owned a second fine home. Tragically, en route across the Atlantic, their ship sank in a storm. The children were swept from their mother's arms as they struggled for their lives. Somehow, the mother managed to stay afloat and was rescued by a lifeboat.

Mrs. Spafford reached Europe and had to immediately get word back to her husband about their terrible loss. She was able to send just two words by Marconi wireless—*SAVED ALONE.*

Devastated, the husband booked passage on another ship to Europe. He asked the captain to let him know when his ship passed over the watery grave of his children. When that moment arrived, he slipped to his stateroom and, in a moment of heartbreaking inspiration, penned words that would be treasured by generations of believers:

> When peace, like a river, attendeth my way,
> When sorrows like sea billows roll—
> Whatever my lot, Thou hast taught me to say,
> It is well, it is well with my soul.

Well, when those two grieving parents met again, they sold their Paris home and decided to travel to Palestine and establish an orphanage. They were able to build it near the Damascus Gate of the wall of Old Jerusalem. It was their way of working through their great sorrow and creating a memorial for their children. The Spaffords also founded the American Colony Hotel just outside the city wall.

That orphanage and that hotel continue to this day. It was there in the American Colony Hotel in the early sixties that I met the Spaffords' eighty-two-year-old daughter. Bertha Spafford Vester was one of two children born to those grieving parents after their loss.

Our interesting conversation led me some years later to contact Lowell Thomas. Mr. Thomas, the well-known news commentator, had known the Spaffords well and became a benefactor of their orphanage in Jerusalem—now called the Spafford Children's Clinic. It was he who wrote the bestselling book about the Spafford story.

About seventeen years ago, I asked Lowell Thomas to speak at our It Is Written partnership weekend in Los Angeles. This celebrated news analyst of a past generation gave a splendid address. But that's not what I remember most. It was something that happened as we stood in the buffet line before dinner. He suggested that I and It Is Written take over the management and financial support of this famed Spafford Children's Clinic in Jerusalem.

I was honored by the offer, of course, and contacted one of the nearby world divisions of the church to consider this opportunity. I learned that Loma Linda Medical Center had joined other U.S. medical centers in America in sending physicians on a rotating basis to the Spafford Center. It seemed to me that any such foothold of influence in that strategic multiracial and multireligious center would be a prize.

However, it soon became evident that we could not use It Is Written dollars for this project. These funds had been given for the specific purpose of television ministry. There were other serious concerns that forced us to turn down Lowell Thomas's offer. Mr. Thomas, then in his eighties, graciously accepted the decision and turned to other means of support for his long-time project. I will always remember and appreciate this man for his offer and his vision for that very special memorial to four children lost at sea.

Another very memorable person comes to mind. Did you know that J. C. Penney was converted to Christ while a patient at Battle Creek Sanitarium and Hospital? It happened shortly after the 1929 stock market crash, which proved to be very traumatic for him. He came to the Kellogg institution in order to recover his emotional balance.

Because of his highly stressed condition, Mr. Penney was watched around the clock. But one morning he managed to slip out of his room undetected. He began wandering around the halls. He happened onto a group of nurses in their morning worship singing "God Will Take Care of You."

Those words and that song touched something

very deep inside him; something very fundamental was awakened. Mr. Penney always looked back on that encounter as the beginning of his conversion to Christ.

In later years, I asked him to appear on our television program to tell his story. We were filming our programs in New York City at the time. Mr. Penney, always the punctual businessman, found his way to the entrance of our 94th Street studio a little bit early for his nine-o'clock appointment. As it happened, that day, I was a little bit late for my usual eight-o'clock start of my taping day. We met on the sidewalk in front of the studio. He took one look at me, rushing up with my briefcase in hand, and said, with a chuckle, "Vandeman, you are late."

Our program with Mr. Penney went well. And that day we began a very pleasant friendship that lasted several years. All JCPenney stores across the nation were notified to watch our program featuring their board chairman. It was an interesting moment—a little different from the normal promotion given to *It Is Written*.

My last visit with Mr. Penney occurred in Phoenix, Arizona. He attended one of our follow-up meetings. We found him a comfortable wicker armchair in which to sit. And I made the mistake of asking him to speak for *a moment or two*. But he went on and on. Bless his heart, we all understood.

Another "early on" experience was a sheer providential opening. I've always been interested in the science of astronomy—not astrology, you understand, but rather the study of the glory of the heavens. And I wanted very much to be able to share the wonders of the created universe in some visual way with our television audience. At one point, I heard that someone had made some very unusual time-lapse photographs of the heavens, photographs that dramatized the movements of heavenly bodies. But I didn't know where they might be. So I began checking every source I could think of. I visited the radio telescope in Manchester, England, and observatories throughout America.

Then one day I discovered that the man I was searching for was Dr. Leroy Sibly, who lived less than a mile from my office in Washington, D.C. Can you imagine! I quickly located his address and found him packing up to move to Florida! (And he apparently had no plans to leave a forwarding address.)

Dr. Sibly had actually spoken at a number of Adventist colleges through the years. When I told him what I hoped to do through television, he was quite appreciative and friendly. And then this generous man reached into a box and pulled out the film footage of the heavens that documented movements as no one else had done. Here were scenes, the like of which did not exist anywhere else. And Dr. Sibly gave me this priceless footage for use in our ministry.

What Dr. Sibly had captured was the perspective of the earth in its twenty-four-hour rotation around the sun. He had condensed this celestial movement through time-lapse photography to three minutes. That is what he placed in my hands. And it was a cherished possession for *It Is Written*, featured on several special science-and-the-Bible programs.

It's always a memorable moment when our God works to prepare an individual for a vital responsibility many years before his influence is needed. Robert Gentry was such a man. He worked as a senior research engineer at the Martin Marietta Company in Orlando, Florida, and carried a top-secret security clearance for his assignments.

Like many scientists, Robert Gentry was committed to the theory of evolution. But one day in the 1960s, while watching television at his home in Orlando, Florida, he happened on an *It Is Written* program that dealt with the subject of Creation. And this man began to wonder about many of the things he'd been taught.

I was able to get in touch with Robert and his wife, Pat, and we had long and serious discussions. They had made a commitment to Jesus Christ and His Word. But their newfound faith seemed to be at war with the evolutionary convictions they held about the origin of life. I remember wondering at the time if God might be calling this brilliant young mind to defend the biblical account of creation within a scientific world thoroughly entrenched in the evolutionary system of thought.

I thank God that Robert Gentry and his wife have since then been able to make new discoveries that harmonized the biblical picture of Creation with what they knew to be scientifically true. (To be fair, let me say that equally faithful Christian teachers of science may have a diversity of convictions concerning a relatively recent Creation versus a longer time of gradual change.)

In these two or three paragraphs, I can't do justice to the evidence Robert Gentry uncovered. Suffice it to say that his book, *Creation's Tiny Mystery*, documents discoveries that have challenged long-held scientific assumptions. Even Dr. Albert Ghiorso, a distinguished atomic scientist who worked on the Manhattan Project, told Robert Gentry that he could not contest his conclusions. I would certainly recommend your reading *Creation's Tiny Mystery* if you're interested in the subject. (For further information, you may write: Earth Science Associates, P.O. Box 12067, Knoxville, TN 37912-0067.)

A choice memory tugs at my heart every time it comes to mind. I hope you'll understand my sharing it. So often I have wondered how effective my ministry to a wide television audience has been to the people closest at hand when we tape the programs—the technical staff in our studio. About twenty-five individuals, technicians from the Los Angeles area with expertise in various aspects of video production, are all connected by headsets to the director as the programs are produced.

After one particular message had been given, the two camera operators nearest me said, "Pastor, we could scarcely keep your face in focus because of *tears that blinded our eyes.*"

Evidently God works in the studio as well as in the homes of millions of receptive souls.

Thank God.

Now two people among the many who found a memorable experience through the *It Is Written* program.

Nellie and I first met James and Kitty Quick at the Ohio camp meeting in Mt. Vernon. They were attending with their entire family. We discovered that they had been watching our program for a number of years and had been deeply impressed with the messages they had heard. What a joy it was to meet this precious family.

James had been an AT&T executive for a number of years. But after his decision to follow his conscience, he arranged for an early retirement. Then both he and his oldest son chose Southern Missionary College as a place to equip themselves for the ministry. Would you believe it! Both father and son attended the college—and graduated together. That was a first in that institution's history.

Afterward, five different state conferences vied with each other as to who should get James Quick—this towering gem of a leader now trained as a minister.

That's one precious couple with a continuing influence in the cause of God whom I wish everyone reading this book could meet.

Another memorable couple shows how quality

persons can be helpful to the church, not by leaving their place of employment, but by finding a new role within it. David and Jean Aldridge are a good example. They began attending church after viewing *It Is Written*.

David has held a highly technical position as head of the Flight Trainers Engineering Division of the navy and now, he is involved with the nation's highly technical weaponry arsenal at Ridgecrest, California, the City of Scientists. Jean has been a high-school teacher in the business education department.

The pastor of the district where David and Jean live considers them his essential associates and feels that losing them would be unthinkable. David organizes church ministry for the pastor, leads in much of the business of the church, and preaches when appropriate. He also trains lay church leaders in the art of management.

Jean Aldridge summarizes the entire church experience, including benefits to their lovely family, in these words: "Our youngest daughter, Allison, joined with us, and our oldest daughter, Chrystal, and her husband, Craig, are also members. Our lifestyle has changed. Status is not so important anymore, and making money is no longer the main topic of conversation. Our church is now the center of our lives. We praise God for this rich and wonderful blessing."

In all the choice moments that have providentially come to me through the years, I can think of but one to close this final chapter.

Fifty-seven years ago, after our wedding ceremony, I traveled with Nellie, my lifelong com-
panion and sweetheart, from South Bend,
Indiana, north to my uncle's cabin on Lake
Michigan for our honeymoon. But on the way
we wanted to make a special stop in Battle
Creek, Michigan. We spent the night at the
Battle Creek Sanitarium and Hospital, where
the manager kindly entertained us and sent
us on our way the next morning after a tasty
breakfast.

We then drove to the Battle Creek Oak Hill
Cemetery. We came with flowers in our hands
that morning, the wedding flowers that were still
fresh in the crisp October air. We wanted to lay
them on the grave of the Lord's last-day mes-
senger, Ellen G. White.

Some of you may have visited this historic
spot—situated only a little way beyond the cemetery entrance. There, within an enclosure of a
stone railing, stands a fifteen-foot granite obelisk, surrounded by the family graves. Nellie and
I stood there a few moments in silence and then
laid our flowers on the grave marked "Mother."
Then we stood back, arm in arm, and read the
inscription.

The name *White* was chiseled prominently on
the face of this obelisk. Also carved there was
that inspiring promise found in Daniel, the
twelfth chapter, verse 3.

And they that be wise shall shine as the bright-
ness of the firmament; and they that turn many

to righteousness as the stars for ever and ever.

Nellie and I vowed that *"turning many to right-eousness"* would be our deepest desire and our fondest dream as we looked to the future.

Has that dream been accomplished? I certainly hope that, by God's grace, it has. But my greatest dream is focused still farther ahead. I look to that day when all of us, without one missing, will sit with the lovely Jesus on the peaceful shore of the River of Life, when we will listen as we hear that incomparable voice, like the sound of many waters, declare, *"Enter thou into the joy of thy Lord."*

Reward enough for us all—wouldn't you say?